Unlocking the Power of Glyphs

Incredibly Powerful Glyphs That Can Change Your Life

by Jean Logan, Ph.D.

Copyright © 2008 by Jean Logan
Third Edition 2019

All rights reserved. No part of this book may be reproduced or utilized in any form or by any means, electronic or mechanical, including photocopying and recording or by any information storage and retrieval system, without permission in writing from the publisher.

Published by Holy Ground Farm, Inc.

Cover design by Bull's-Eye Creative Communications
Book design by Jill Anderson, www.JillLynnDesign.com
Chakra Drawings by Dan Winner

ISBN-13: 978-1-62890-839-8
ISBN-10: 1-60530-170-1

Library of Congress Control Number: 2008934021

Printed in China through Four Colour Imports USA

1 3 5 7 9 10 8 6 4 2

Acknowledgement

My sincerest gratitude to Dean Logan, whose belief in me and support of my work, made this book possible.

Table of Contents

INTRODUCTION 9
UNLOCKING THE POWER OF GLYPHS 11
THE GLYPHS 15

Glyph 01	Clearing of Meridians	17
Glyph 02	Trust	21
Glyph 03	Ancestral Influences	25
Glyph 04	Detoxification	29
Glyph 05	Fear	33
Glyph 06	Anger – Resentment – Frustration	37
Glyph 07	Guilt – Shame – Embarrassment	41
Glyph 08	Release All Blocks	45
Glyph 09	Chakras	49
Glyph 10	Anti-Bacterial/Viral	53
Glyph 13	Grief – Sadness – Depression	57
Glyph 14	Relief from Tension and Anxiety	61
Glyph 15	Parasites in Humans or Animals	65
Glyph 16	Release Vows	69
Glyph 17	Focus and Organization	73

Glyph 18	Heartache – Fear of Abandonment	77
Glyph 19	Bites from Insects	81
Glyph 23	Repair Damaged Nerves	85
Glyph 25	Headaches – Energy Release	89
Glyph 26	Course Correct and Alignment	93
Glyph 29	Abundance Gene Activation – Reconnect DNA	97
Glyph 30	General Balancing	101
Glyph 46	Love Frequency	105
Glyph 50	Reaching Out	109
Glyph 52	People of the World	113
Glyph 55	Sever Agreement of Pain	117
Glyph 56	Removing Blocks	121
Glyph 61	Remove Attached Entities	125
Glyph 73	Cellular Repair	129
Glyph 82	Courage, Confidence and Joy	133
Appendix A	Glyph Chart	137
Appendix B	Locating the Chakras	139
Appendix C	Dowsing	141
Appendix D	AcuTapping	145
Appendix E	Suggested Reading	147
Appendix F	The Grand Invocation	149
Appendix G	Disclaimer	151

Dedication

The work in this manual is dedicated to all those who are seeking. May they find their answers.

This book and the glyphs contained herein are empowered with the violet flame of St. Germain. St. Germain has attached an aspect of himself to each manual including those electronically reproduced.

Message from St. Germain.

"Listen to your heart. Know that I am with you always. My love is genuine. Hold the flame of that love to your heart. See the Divine in all your brothers and sisters. Know that your path is chosen. Mark the time for it will come to pass. I want you to understand that your duty is to the beloved I Am Presence in all things. I see your sorrows and know the love in your heart. Contemplate the meaning of all you do to see that it corresponds with the purpose for your being here."

All of the proceeds from this manual are used to help our work with disadvantaged children. If your friends would like a copy, please encourage them to buy their own copy or make a donation to cover any copies given out to others. Your spiritual integrity in this matter is very much appreciated.

The holder of a valid receipt for the purchase of this manual has permission to have copies made of any of the images inside the manual.

Many blessings and enjoy the use of these glyphs.

Introduction

First of all, I want to explain what a glyph is. According to Webster's Dictionary, a glyph is:

"A symbol that conveys information nonverbally."

One internet definition site defined it as "a symbol or character, especially one that has been incised or carved out in a stone surface like the characters of the ancient Maya writing system."

A few years ago I received an e-mail from a friend that contained a glyph. The glyph was a small drawing of some type of insect with a wavy line around it. The author of the glyph wrote under it, "Restoring Divine DNA Blueprint." She also wrote next to it and under it, "Star Glyph to remove Parasitic DNA Mutation that invites in entities and is an energetic link to Fear Programming. This glyph restores the DNA. Please circulate widely and reproduce freely—(Do not Alter) use with integrity. Humans were DNA altered by genetic engineering at the time of the fall of Atlantis and Babylon. A parasitic mutation attached (recessive gene) to DNA making humans susceptible to entities." I have included a copy of this glyph below.

There was the name, Judith K. Moore, and her e-mail address on the page. I have always been fascinated by glyphs and this one was certainly no exception. I printed the page and cut out the picture of the glyph. Then I thought "All right, what should I do with it?" It said "Use with integrity", but I wondered, "How?" At that moment I either decided or was guided to place the drawing on my solar plexus. Immediately there was a tremendous amount of activity in my liver. I would call it a level two pain on a one to ten scale. It certainly was not enough to have me running down the street screaming, but definitely very noticeable. This went on for several minutes, after which I did a little energy healing on the area. When I tried this again the next day, nothing happened. My son, Patrick, tried the glyph in the same manner, but did not notice anything. I wasn't sure what it was all about, but I thought "Whatever it was, I had it, and now it's gone." I also thought "Whoever created this glyph with this much power, I can do that too!"

A couple of years before that incident, while I was meditating, I saw a vision of a paper with writing on it. I felt that this meant I should try guided writing. The next day I went out on our deck with a notebook and pen in hand. I did my best to clear my mind. I began writing whatever thoughts came to me. The first page was just gibberish. As I began the second page I received this: "We are beings of Light and we are here to guide you." What followed was a profound writing from nature spirits. I continued this practice and find I am now able to readily communicate with unseen benevolent guides as well as our Source. Let me point out that I am a conscious channel and do not go into a trance to receive messages.

Following my introduction to Judith Moore's glyph, I asked my guides how glyphs are created. They gave me a brief review of how this is done. Then I set about making some elementary glyphs of my own, with just some simple words: "Energy", "Industriousness", "Joy", and so forth. These efforts achieved no noticeable results. I then decided that in order for me to obtain such things as joy, I would need to remove the negative emotional baggage standing in the way. I realized the same would be true for everyone.

It was about that time that I received a call from my friend Kathy. She told me that several days earlier she had taken her dogs' glass drinking bowl out of the dishwasher while it was still hot, placed it on the floor, and without thinking poured cold water into the bowl. It was like it exploded, she told me, with a piece of glass being driven deep into her foot. Although she was able to remove the glass, the foot was now badly infected: inflamed with considerable swelling, painful, oozing, and had a foul odor. Although Kathy is a registered nurse, she knows the importance of avoiding antibiotics unless they are absolutely necessary. Knowing my background in various healing modalities, she asked me if I knew of anything that could help her foot. My first thought was a type of antibiotic herb. But then I decided I would create a glyph and program it to destroy bacteria. I asked Kathy if she would be willing to participate in a little experiment, to which she agreed. I created two glyphs, one that would take care of the bacteria, and a second glyph to speed healing, then e-mailed them to Kathy. She e-mailed me back the next day. "I really think my glyphs are working! I put them face down on top of my dressing, bacteria killers first and then cell renewal. My foot was swollen, red and oozing to the point where I had to change the bandages at least four or five times a day. The next morning, the redness was gone, the swelling was way down, the wound look cleaner, and there was practically no drainage. Also, it doesn't burn and hurt. Wow!!!" When I spoke to her a couple of weeks later, she said the wound was almost completely healed.

I continued to create glyphs, concentrating on designing them to remove the negative emotions that seem to plague so many of us. All my life I have been troubled with depression and fear. I was sure that removing these disabling energies was an important step on my path. Using myself as a guinea pig, I found that the glyphs easily and effectively began removing more and more of the emotional burdens I had been carrying. Instead of waking up in the morning feeling depressed, I found myself feeling lighter, more vibrant, and glad to be alive during these exciting times. Being very sensitive to energy, I could feel the glyphs working. I created a glyph to remove heavy metals and other toxic matter from the body. My first efforts left me with a headache; but finally I created a detoxification glyph that worked with no side effects. Again, I could feel the sensation of something being drawn out of the body.

We are all a part of the energy of our Source. This means that within us lies all the power we need to heal ourselves and to draw to us everything we desire. Our one failing, however, is that we don't believe we possess that power. All the doubts, fears and negative programming we have accumulated over the years are blocking our way. We may realize this, but that doesn't make these obstacles go away. These negative beliefs stick to us like glue. There are those who would suggest counseling to rid ourselves of this excess baggage. Although counseling has its place, it can be expensive, not to mention the time spent sitting in someone's office while they attempt to dredge out all of the deep, dark secrets that go all the way back to before we can remember. Others might suggest past life regression to delve into horrendous lifetimes of pain and torture. Again, this might be helpful, but when we stop to realize that we have had hundreds of lifetimes, we can see that may not be a very practical answer. Prayer Glyphs can remove much of whatever is holding us back; no digging into painful past memories, no expensive counseling. Finally, we have the tools we need to help remove the fear, guilt, sadness, anger, resentment, or whatever else is standing in our way.

The idea of drawings on a piece of paper being so powerful that they can kill bacteria or remove emotional blockages may seem difficult to believe. We must think for a moment of the power of the Word and the power of prayer. The glyphs contain both of these. The amount of energy here is immeasurable by any of our standards. To those who do not believe this is possible, I quote the words of Albert Einstein, *"The most beautiful thing we can experience is the mysterious. It is the source of all true art and science. . . . He who can no longer pause to wonder and stand rapt in awe, is as good as dead; his eyes are closed."*

Unlocking the Power of Glyphs

The glyphs in this manual are a form of spiritual energy, a language of Light. Each glyph invokes a powerful prayer directed at a specific thing for a specific purpose. It has been proven, many times over, that prayer heals. Much of the information for these glyphs was given to me by Source. I was told to write this book by Source. When I asked Source, *"By what name should I call you in the book?"* I was told, *"By my name, Source Energy, God, Jehovah, Creator or Christ. It is all the same."*

These glyphs are energized by Source and highly evolved spiritual beings during a sacred ceremony at a sacred site high in the Blue Ridge Mountains of North Carolina. The energy from the glyph, together with prayers and intentions of the user, form a strong bond that enhances the body's ability to resolve inner-conflict, release negative patterns, and mend old wounds. Every person is an extension of Source Energy and, therefore, is unlimited. As a part of our Source, there is nothing, nor anyone, who can prevent us from achieving happiness, health and abundance for ourselves.

Using the Glyphs

When using these glyphs, it is important to focus on gratitude, because gratitude elevates our vibration and makes us more receptive to healing energy. Every morning, make a list of all the things you are grateful for. Focus on these thoughts and verbally release any negative emotions. Sound can be very helpful in releasing.

It is important to see ourselves as already free of any physical or emotional problems. Thinking about or talking about our perceived problems, only serves to re-create the negative energy patterns that prevent us from restoring ourselves to the perfect being we were created to be. See yourself the way you want to be; you will be guided in that direction. It is important to recognize that we create our own reality.

Every thought creates a flow of energy. We can literally create, or draw to us, emotional or physical illness by our negative thinking. In the same manner, we can change that by elevating our thoughts to be more positive. This positive change in our attitude can create a powerful transformation. Although the glyphs can help us release emotions we are holding within us, they cannot prevent us from accumulating more of the same unless we are willing to make these changes.

Start out by using one glyph at a time. Remember, you are working with energy. Don't try to get too many things going at once. After you have used them for a while, you can experiment. Some glyphs may work in just ten or fifteen minutes, but it is best if you can leave them on overnight. Glyph 4, *Detoxification*, and Glyph 10, *Anti-Bacterial*, should always be left on overnight. All glyphs can, and should be used repeatedly. Many of the problems that are holding us back are buried deep within us—like the layers of an onion. You peel-off one layer at a time, revealing another one underneath. This continues until all the layers are removed. Be patient! It may take some time, but work with the glyphs. Sometimes you may feel something happening, especially if you are very sensitive to what is going on within your body. Other times you will not notice anything. That does not mean they are not working—the energy is very subtle. The longer you work with the glyphs, the better the results you will achieve. You will find a generous supply of these glyphs in the manual, and they can prove to be very useful. Use a fabric tape or some type of medical tape to hold them in place. Experiment!

Although the energy from the glyphs will move throughout the body, better results can often be obtained from placing the glyph on the chakra of the area where the problem is located. A picture showing the location of the chakras is included as Appendix B. These glyphs, as well as other types of energy healing, work best when the body is completely relaxed. Most of them can be used anywhere on the body. The emotional-release glyphs will be helpful on most of the chakras, and especially over organs and glands.

We can harbor emotional blockages anywhere, even in our feet and toes—a possible cause of corns, bunions, etc. Try putting the *Detoxification* glyphs on the bottoms of your feet, where many reflexology and acupuncture meridian points are located. This is best done by covering a shoe insert with a sheet of the glyphs, taping-down the corners, then inserting this into a loose-fitting sock, which is then worn throughout the night. If the sensation is too intense and keeps you from sleeping, remove them and try again another night. The intensity will decrease as negative emotions or toxins are removed from your body. Do not underestimate the importance of an affirmation or prayer. If you have a prayer or affirmation that feels better to you than the one in this manual, by all means say the one that you think is more meaningful. Sound is very effective in releasing pent up emotions.

Be sure to place the glyphs on the chakras on the back as well as the front. The chakras on the back may address past life issues. When I was dowsing (see Appendix C) on which glyphs to use, I was frequently directed to place the *Abundance* glyph on various chakras on my back. I believe this was to remove vows of poverty, or other financially-restrictive blocks from past lives.

Arthritis and rheumatism are usually caused by an excessive build-up of anger and resentment. Do your best to uncover areas of your life where you are holding resentment. The glyph for resentment will help. Good results can often be obtained by placing a glyph on the chakra in the area where there is a problem, continuing then with detoxification glyphs. When we come to realize that we create our own reality, we find there is little cause for resentment.

Ensure that you drink plenty of water daily—at least sixty-four ounces. Coffee, tea and carbonated beverages do not count as most of these are diuretics, as are some herbal teas. To perform at its best, the body needs to be well hydrated. Dehydration can cause any number of health problems.

Eat plenty of fresh fruits and vegetables. Avoid the use of sugar since it has been proven to depress the immune system and drain your energy. Also avoid the use of artificial sweeteners; they are toxic to the body and can have the adverse effect of causing a craving for carbohydrates. Processed foods are empty calories and processed oils are known to be toxic. Practice deep-breathing exercises. A person on a healing path requires plenty of oxygen.

Get plenty of exercise. Exercise relieves depression and stimulates digestion. If you are one of those who hate to exercise, take up dancing or join a hiking club.

Release judgment of others. As we judge others, so are we judged by others. We hold our judgements within us, which will prevent us from healing. The one we judge most often is our own self. It is important to not be so hard on ourselves. Love yourself, warts and all!

It is also important to love unconditionally. We find this to be most difficult when dealing with family members, close friends, and those we deal with most often. We place expectations upon them, feeling they should live up to those expectations. Again, the one we have the most difficulty loving unconditionally is our own self. How then can we love others if we don't love ourselves? We must learn to practice acceptance when we find ourselves in a situation we cannot change. We don't make mistakes, we don't do things wrong; we learn from our life experiences. Remember, each of us is on our own spiritual path and we all have the right to make our own choices. We don't need to concern ourselves with the choices that others make; we have no way of knowing what their path is.

Avoid criticism and complaining. This can attract and hold negative energy in your body. This negative energy can lead to illness and keep you from manifesting what you desire. One good book to help you is *Ask and it is Given*, by Esther and Jerry Hicks. It explains the "cause and effect" and how we can change ourselves to bring more harmony into our lives.

Work to resolve fear-related problems. Fear is like a magnet; it attracts to you whatever it is that you may fear. As I look back, I realize that my entire life was controlled by fear. You name it, I was afraid of it: insects, water, traveling in an airplane. I was afraid to go anywhere, do anything, or have any fun. As I slowly released all my pent-up emotions, I found my life expanding into many new areas.

Another great way to release negative emotions is by tapping on various acupuncture points while verbally making a statement about releasing the problem. This technique is especially effective when we are aware of what the emotion is that is troubling us. It is also effective when we suddenly remember something painful from our past. This is an indication that the emotion is ready to be released. Using the motion of tapping plus the sound of your voice is very powerful. This technique was pioneered by Dr. Roger Callahan and others, and is called by different names including Emotional Thought Field Therapy and Acutapping. At Appendix D you will find a description of one form of this technique that is very effective. This particular method is presented by Dr. "Buzz" Johnson.

Other resources for this method are two great books, *Instant Emotional Healing* by Peter Lambrou and George Pratt and *Freedom From Fear Forever* by James Durlasher.

Glyphs may be used on pets. My dog, Roscoe, is afraid of thunder and lightening. He trembles and shakes at the slightest rumble in the distance. He always awakens me any time there is a storm at night. I put the glyph for fear on his back solar plexus and he falls asleep without a problem.

Putting a piece of tape over the glyph on the animal's back will help to keep it in place. Glyphs are best used when a pet is sleeping. A picture showing various chakra locations on a dog is included in Appendix B. The chakras for cats can be found in the same locations as they are found for dogs.

At Appendix A you will find a chart which provides assistance in the effective use of glyphs. For relief of some types of headaches, try Glyph 25, *Congestion*. Place on the ajna chakra (between the eyebrows), for five to ten minutes, then using Glyph 30, *General Balancing*, for ten to fifteen minutes followed by Glyph 4, *Detoxification*. (The detoxification glyph should remain in place for a much longer period of time than the other two glyphs). Drink plenty of water.

One of the most exquisite results of using these glyphs is the ability to remove inhibitions, sexual and otherwise. I can attest to this myself. My childhood was a veritable minefield of taboos. I had more sexual inhibitions than an auditorium full of nuns (Sorry Sisters, just joking). After continued use of the glyphs, you may find that you can assault your lover with wild abandon; it's great "doing it," with the lights on; you can enjoy touching and being touched; you don't need to keep your naked body hidden; you will feel beautiful even without clothing. These glyphs can save a lot of marriages.

A friend of mine living in Peru, has a housekeeper who contracted Dengue Fever, and had been in the hospital for over a week. I e-mailed Glyph 10, *Anti-Bacterial*, to him. He printed them and took the prints to the hospital. He placed one page of them on her back, over the back of the heart chakra. Then he put an individual glyph on both her front solar plexus and her front heart chakra. The next morning her temperature returned to normal, and she was released from the hospital the following day. She told one of the nurses about the glyph, and she was accused of practicing voodoo.

Another friend who was experiencing intense anguish after discovering her husband was having an affair with another woman, found relief from her trauma by stacking the Trust, Abandonment, Depression, Fear, Anxiety, Anger and Sadness glyphs on top of each other, then taping them over her heart chakra.

In another instance, a case of scabies was resolved by taping the glyph for parasites over the affected area.

One day I suddenly developed a very sore throat that included the glands in the front of my neck and went all the way up to under my ears. I cut out several of the *Anti-Bacterial*, Glyph 10, and put one over the area under each ear, one on the front of my throat over the throat chakra, a group of four over my solar plexus, and a group of four on the back of my heart chakra. I could feel it start to work right away, and the next morning my sore throat was completely gone.

One of my contact lenses caused me to experience an eye infection; it was oozing and red. I placed an *Anti-Bacterial* glyph over the eye for a few hours and the infection was resolved. I am stating this as my experience and not advising anyone to do the same. Neither am I advising the use of the glyphs for any serious medical problems or conditions. Seek medical treatment for serious illnesses.

For effective relief from itching under the eye, caused by seasonal allergies, place a strip of the *Detoxification* glyphs on the front of the shin bone, over what will feel like a crevice, of the opposite leg. It may sound strange, but remember, everything is connected.

For the painful bite of an insect such as a yellow jacket or wasp, place the *Insect Bites* glyph over the area as soon as possible. I received a very painful sting on my back. I immediately went in and used the glyph for insect bites and was amazed how quickly it worked. The sooner it is used the better. It is helpful for mosquito bites if used right away. For chiggers, use Glyph 15, *Parasites* and place Glyph 19, *Insect Bites*, on top. In all cases, seek medical attention for life threatening situations, including snake bites. Rattlesnakes and water moccasins are deadly, so don't take any chances. I don't want to even think about getting a snake bite, but if I did, I would use this glyph on the way to the hospital.

When I was troubled with sneezing and a runny nose caused by seasonal allergies, I obtained considerable relief by putting Glyph 4, *Detoxification*, on the ajna chakra, then one under each eye on the cheek bone. Needless to say, this is not something that you will want to wear when going out in public, but it was very effective. It allowed me to get a good night's sleep and I could wear it while working around the house. The real resolution is to strengthen the immune system.

A page of Glyph 4, *Detoxification*, placed over the abdomen, relieved symptoms of digestive distress caused by certain foods. The Detoxification glyphs are also very helpful in relieving pain from sore muscles due to over-exertion. Simply place a strip of the glyphs over the sore area.

You will notice that the numbering of the glyphs is not consecutive. This is because many of the glyphs were created for specific persons who had/have specific problems. Other glyphs were not found appropriate for listing in this manual and will be included in a follow up manual.

The following chart summarizes the appendixes located at the back of the book.

Appendix A	Contains a chart which will prove helpful in deciding which glyph can help with different types of problems or conditions.
Appendix B	Provides information on chakras, and their locations, on both humans and animals.
Appendix C	Contains dowsing charts that can assist you in locating and deciding which glyphs your body needs, and where they should be placed.
Appendix D	AcuTapping to remove present negative emotions from the meridians.
Appendix E	Suggested Readings.
Appendix F	"*The Grand Invocation*," a very powerful affirmation. Consider reciting it daily.
Appendix G	Disclaimer

The Glyphs

The following pages contain a title and explanation page for each glyph followed by pages of the actual glyphs. These glyphs can be used in several ways:

As a whole sheet to place the hands on (to use for 10, 15 minutes or more).

Cut out as a block of four to place under the back of the heart chakra, or any other chakra, while lying down.

Cut with scissors to fit a shoe insert for placing in a large sock to be worn at bedtime.

Cut out individually and taped over a chakra or problem area.

Glyphs can be used on self or others with a surrogate such as a picture, stuffed animal or paper with a protocol. Statement of intention or affirmation is important here.

There really is no wrong way or wrong place to use the glyphs. The glyphs should be cut around the outside of the black wavy border.

If the glyph becomes wet or damaged in any way, discard it.

It is helpful to say the affirmation (or your own prayer or affirmation) out loud, as the words have a positive vibration to them that will be very helpful.

The question arises with any type of healing system, "Do I have to believe in this before it will work?" Belief is a very powerful energy, but it is difficult for a person to believe in something different until they have a convincing experience. If one is open and receptive, the glyphs will work well. If, however, a person has a totally negative attitude toward any kind of healing modality, they put out a powerful energy field of resistance. How much this affects any results depends upon the level of energy their resistance generates. I suggest that no one try to get someone to use these glyphs if they are not interested or have already decided they will not work. The glyphs represent the power of prayer and the power of intention. A positive intention from the user of the glyph intensifies the ability of the glyph to achieve greater results. It is that simple.

From Glyph Users

It is important to understand that these glyphs will help prepare people for the change in energy that we are experiencing in the coming shift.

Many users report good results by using these glyphs remotely. They place their name and location of where the energy should go and place that on a glyph and INTEND the energy be sent to that location.

These are some of the ideas and suggestions from purchases of this glyph manual:

One user reported lying down with a page of Glyph #1 Meridians under her ear helped headaches caused by blockage of this meridian.

Following the work of Masaru Emoto Jeanne Garner printed out the glyph for "Courage, Confidence and Joy" and left it under her water bottle overnight. The next morning, she found that the water had a much more beautiful taste, and for "some reason the day went exceedingly well... the joy part came through, loud and clear." Similar reports from using the Love Glyph #46 under drinking water.

One man wrote to report he was told in a dream to put a page of Remove Blocks to Abundance #29 under his computer. Another stated he got good results putting one of these glyphs in his wallet.

Rev Barbara Grearney said she puts things she is selling on a page of Reaching Out #50 and INTENDS the glyph reach out to bring the buyer to her. She said it works every time. She also reported strong energies and attunements following using the glyphs.

We welcome hearing about your experiences with the glyphs. Go to www.powerglyphsbook.com and put your comments in the Blog section.

glyph **01**

Clearing of Meridians

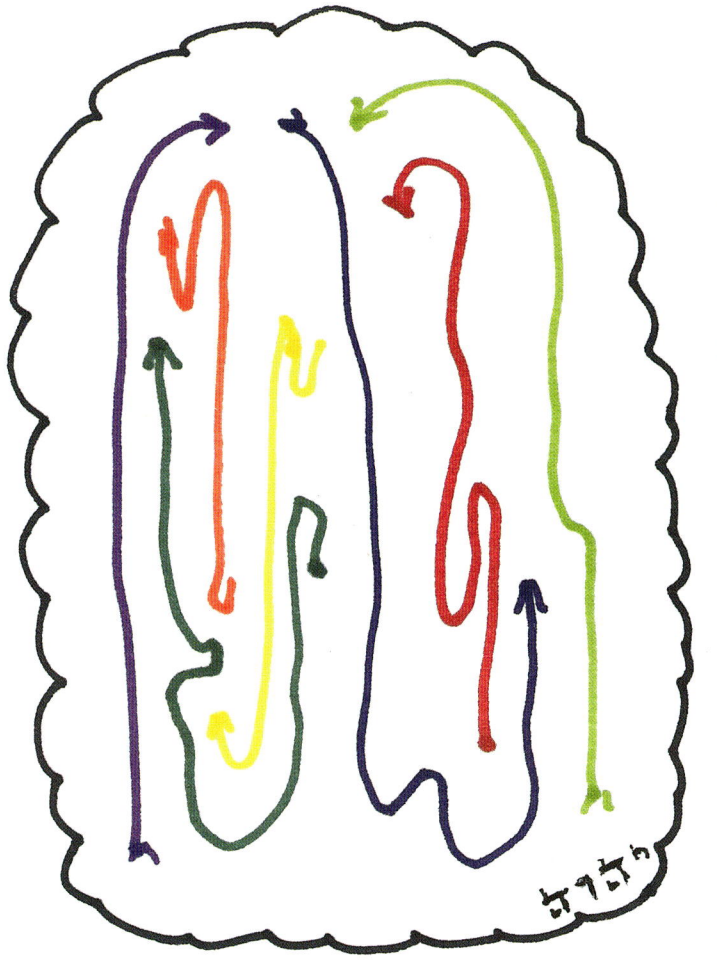

This prayer glyph can clear the acupuncture meridians of constriction and blockages and encourage the movement of energy. You can put your finger tips on the glyph, put them under your feet or place it on any major chakra. Allow at least ten to fifteen minutes.

Suggested Affirmation: With God's helpful loving hands, I clear myself of any and all blockages in my meridians. I see the energy flowing through me with ease. I see myself as healthy and full of energy. I am grateful for the Divine energy that is flowing through me now.

Suggested Affirmation: With God's helpful loving hands, I clear myself of any and all blockages in my meridians. I see the energy flowing through me with ease. I see myself as healthy and full of energy. I am grateful for the Divine energy that is flowing through me now.

Clearing of Meridians

glyph 02

Trust

This prayer glyph can help remove the desire to dominate and control and replace this inclination with trust and patience. It also helps remove the lack of self worth. It then balances the energies of the right and left hemisphere of the brain and assists the body in adjusting to new frequencies. Use on any or all major chakras and both front or back of your navel.

Suggested Affirmation: I release all desire to dominate and control the outcome of any situation. I realize that there is a Divine Plan of which I am a part. I place my trust in the Creator. I intend Divine Light, guidance, and protection as I go throughout each and every day. Thank You God for the guidance I receive.

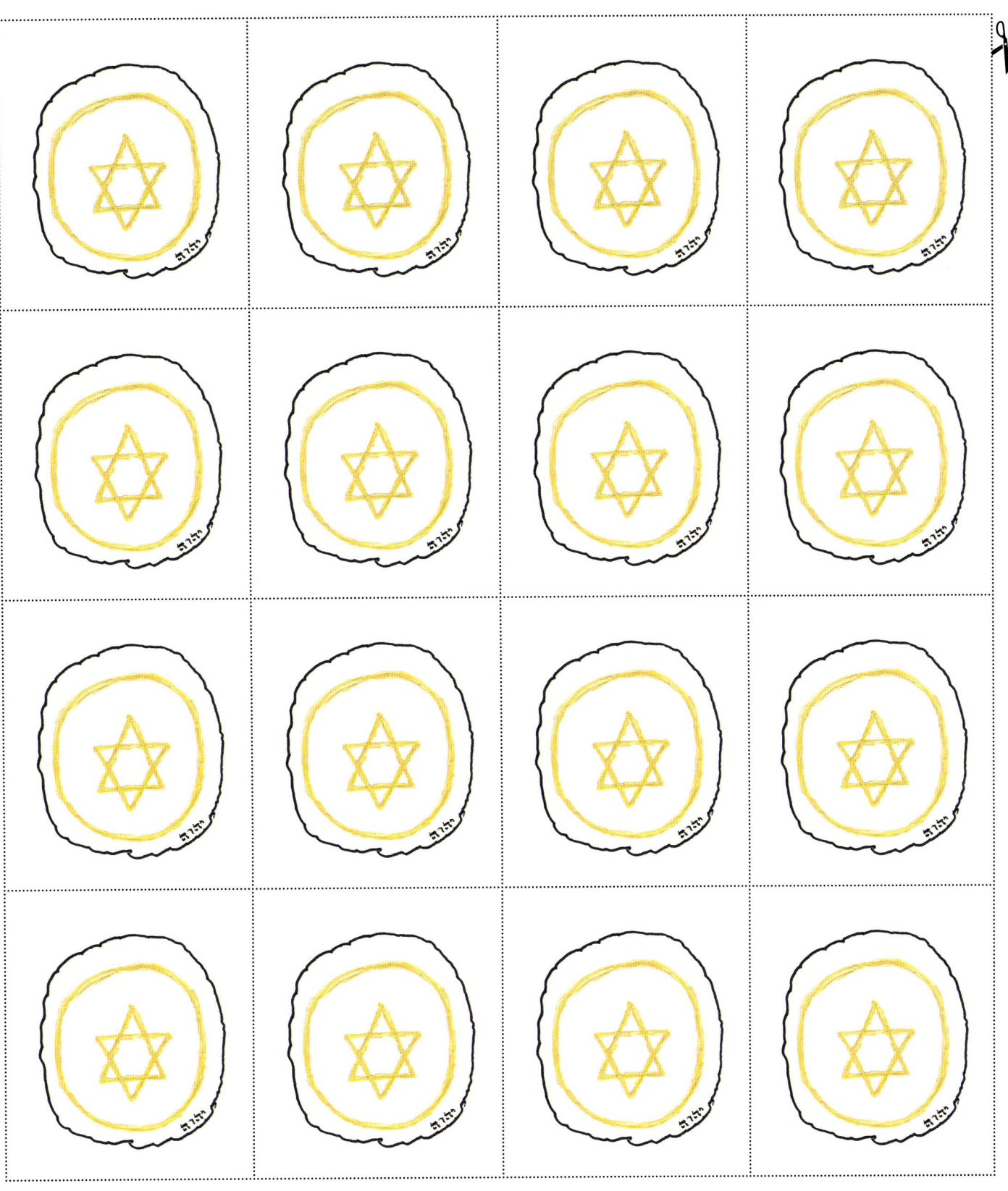

Suggested Affirmation: I release all desire to dominate and control the outcome of any situation. I realize that there is a Divine Plan of which I am a part. I place my trust in the Creator. I intend Divine Light, guidance, and protection as I go throughout each and every day. Thank You God for the guidance I receive.

glyph 03

Ancestral Influences

This prayer glyph provides healing of the ancestral lineage. It is useful for clearing problems passed down from ancestors or problems that are hereditary in nature, as well as problems that are the result of things from past lives. This glyph should be placed on the navel and back of the navel. It can also be used on any of the major chakras, including the back.

Suggested Affirmation: I release myself of any past lives or ancestral lineage that is not for my highest good. I bless all of my ancestors and hold them in the Light.

(Do the following slowly and with intention and sincerity.) I call before me the souls of anyone that I may have harmed in this lifetime or past lifetimes and I sincerely apologize for any harm that I have done to all of you and ask your forgiveness. I release you with the highest love and light.

I call before me anyone who has harmed me in this lifetime or past lifetime and I state sincerely that I forgive you. I release you in light and love.

Call on the keeper of the Akashic Records and ask to have all your negative karma removed.

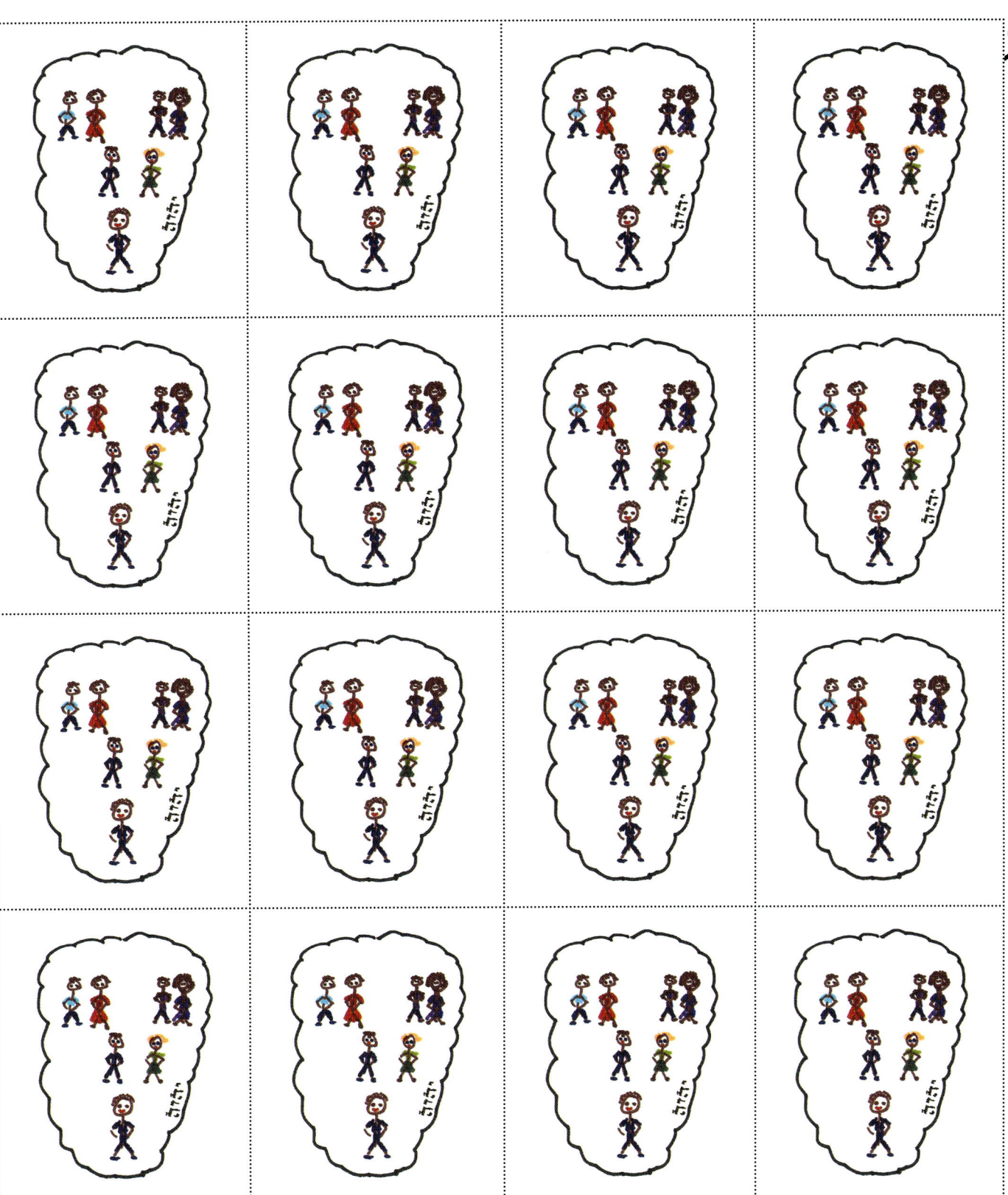

Suggested Affirmation: I release myself of any past lives or ancestral lineage that are not for my highest good. I bless all of my ancestors and hold them in the Light.

glyph 04

Detoxification

Regular use of this prayer glyph can detoxify the physical body and aura. One way to effectively use this glyph is to put it on a shoe insert with some type of tape, put the insert inside a knit booty or large sock, and wear this during the night. If you are a light sleeper, the drawing feeling as it transitions toxins to Light may disturb your sleep. After you use this glyph several times this feeling will diminish. Aching muscles from over exertion can be relieved by placing the glyph over the sore area and leaving it in place for fifteen minutes or more.

Suggested Affirmation: Creator, with Your help and guidance, I release myself from any toxic matter or debris that is affecting my health or my journey to evolve. I see myself as a temple of Your Light and choose a path of wellness.

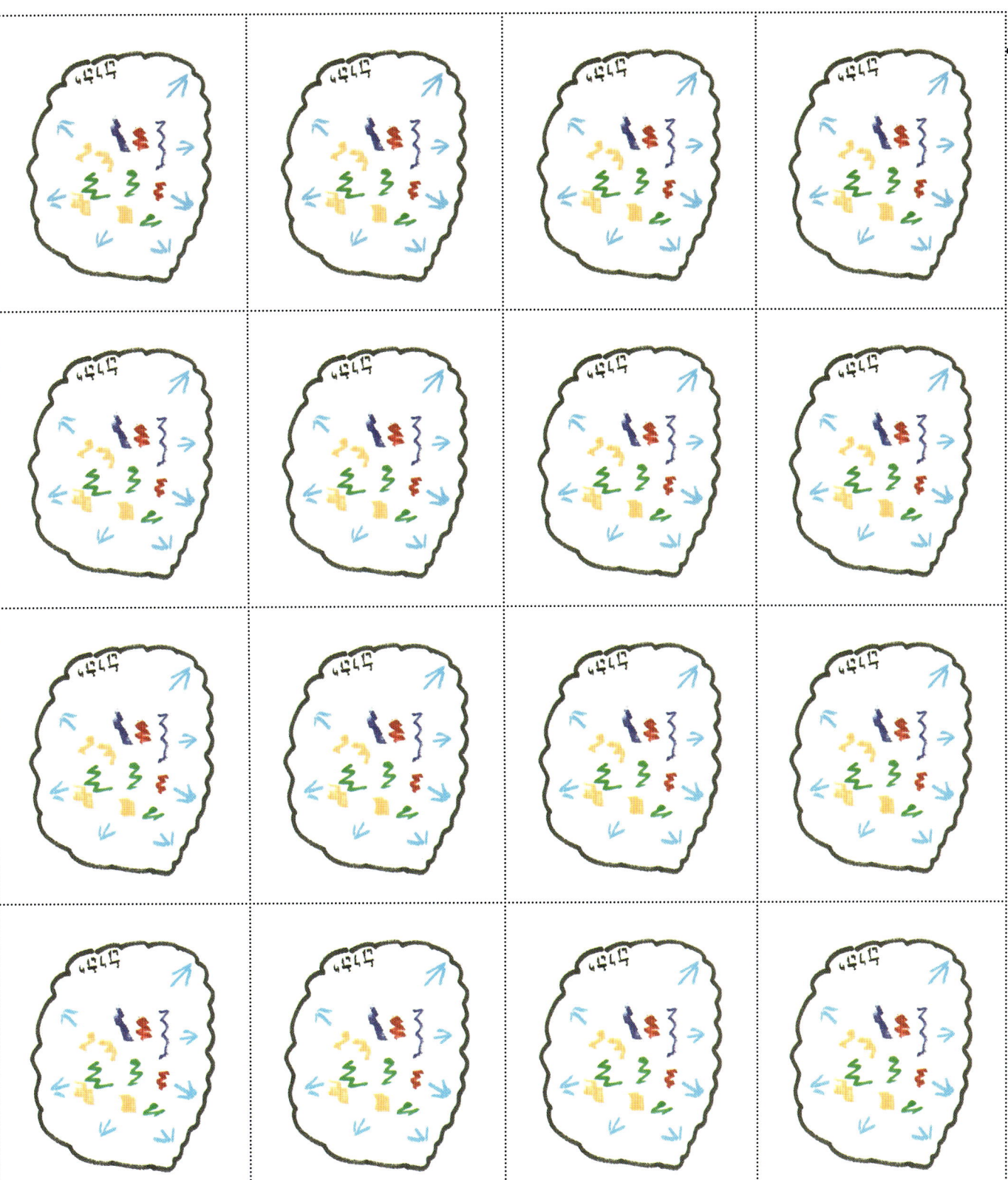

Suggested Affirmation: Creator, with Your help and guidance, I release myself from any toxic matter or debris that is affecting my health or my journey to evolve. I see myself as a temple of Your Light and choose a path of wellness.

glyph **05**

Fear

This prayer glyph can help remove fear from the body and the aura. It can be placed on any major or minor chakra including the back, over the spleen chakra (under the rib cage on the left side), under the liver or back of the navel. As there are many types of fear, this glyph should be used often and in many areas. This glyph can be very effective on dogs that are afraid of thunder and lightning. Place the glyph on the animal's back solar plexus or heart chakra during the storm.

Suggested Affirmation: I release all fear that I have been holding within me. I realize that I have nothing to fear when I trust. I intend Divine Light, guidance, and protection as I go throughout each and every day. Thank You God for everything. I create around myself a self-renewing protective shield that will keep me from harm.

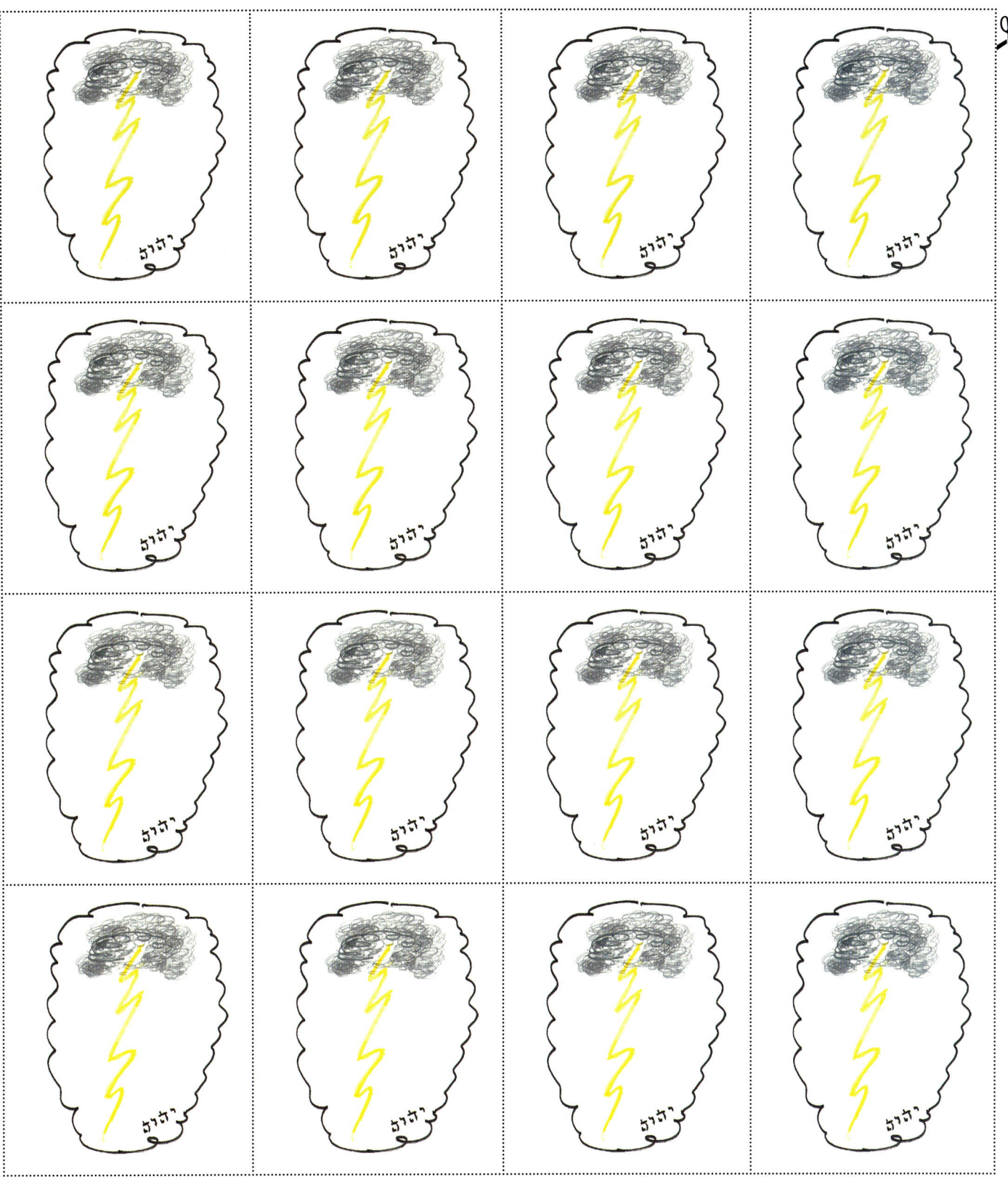

Suggested Affirmation: I release all fear that I have been holding within me. I realize that I have nothing to fear when I trust. I intend Divine Light, guidance, and protection as I go throughout each and every day. Thank You God for everything. I create around myself a self-renewing protective shield that will keep me from harm.

Fear

glyph **06**

Anger Resentment Frustration

This prayer glyph can remove residual anger, resentment and frustration from the body and the aura. This glyph can be used on any major or minor chakra, back of the navel, over the spleen chakra, and under the liver. Another way of using this glyph is to place the hands on a whole sheet of the glyphs. They can also be used the same way under the feet. Leave the hands or feet in place on the glyphs until any sensation stops. If the sensation is too intense to leave the hands on very long, try it again later. This can be used as often as you feel it is necessary.

Suggested Affirmation: I release all anger, resentment and frustration that I have been holding within me. I replace these with love and acceptance. I see myself as loving unconditionally without judgement.

Suggested Affirmation: I release all anger, resentment and frustration that I have been holding within me. I replace these with love and acceptance. I see myself as loving unconditionally without judgement.

Anger – Resentment – Frustration

glyph **07**

Guilt
Shame
Embarrassment

This glyph can remove residual guilt, shame, embarrassment, and humiliation from the body and the aura. This glyph can be used on any major or minor chakra, back of the navel, over the spleen chakra and under the liver. Another way of using this glyph, is to place the hands on the whole sheet of glyphs. They can be used the same way under the feet. Leave the hands or feet in place on the glyphs until any sensation stops.

Suggested Affirmation: I release all guilt, shame, humiliation and embarrassment from my body and my auric field. I see myself in the Light. I release anything from within me that is not love and Light. I am grateful for the release and healing that is taking place within me.

43   Guilt – Shame – Embarrassment

Suggested Affirmation: I release all guilt, shame, humiliation and embarrassment from my body and my auric field. I see myself in the Light. I release anything from within me that is not love and Light. I am grateful for the release and healing that is taking place within me.

glyph **08**

Release All Blocks

This prayer glyph can remove blocks that prevent the Light of God from reaching our inner being. This glyph can be used on any major or minor chakra, back of the navel, over the spleen chakra, and under the liver. Another way of using this glyph, is to place the hands on a whole sheet of the glyphs. They can be used the same way under the feet. Leave the hands or feet in place on the glyphs until any sensation stops.

Suggested Affirmation: I release all that is blocking me from being totally in the Light. I see and hold Light at the center of my being. I am one with God, therefore, I am the Light.

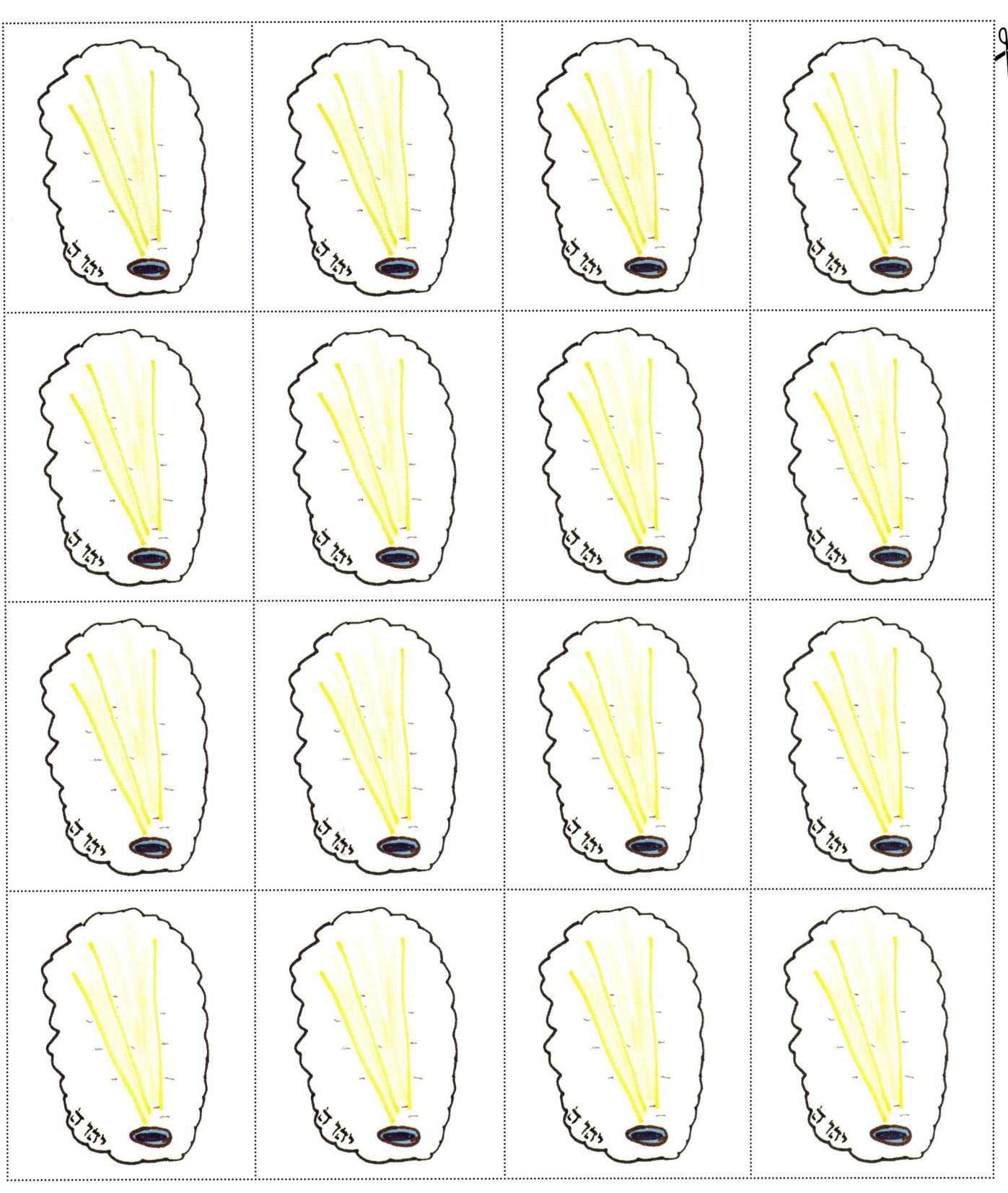

Suggested Affirmation: I release all that is blocking me from being totally in the Light. I see and hold Light at the center of my being. I am one with God, therefore, I am the Light.

glyph **09**

Chakras

This prayer glyph can clear and align all major chakras and the navel chakra, which is a minor chakra. Place on the solar plexus and/or any major chakra. Leave in place at least fifteen minutes or overnight.

Suggested Affirmation: Creator, with Your help and guidance, I align all of my chakras, clear them of any afflictions and repair any disfigurement starting with my base chakra, moving up to my sacral chakra, my solar plexus, my heart chakra, my throat chakra, my third eye and my crown chakra. I see them restored to perfect balance. Thank You Creator for Your divine guidance and assistance.

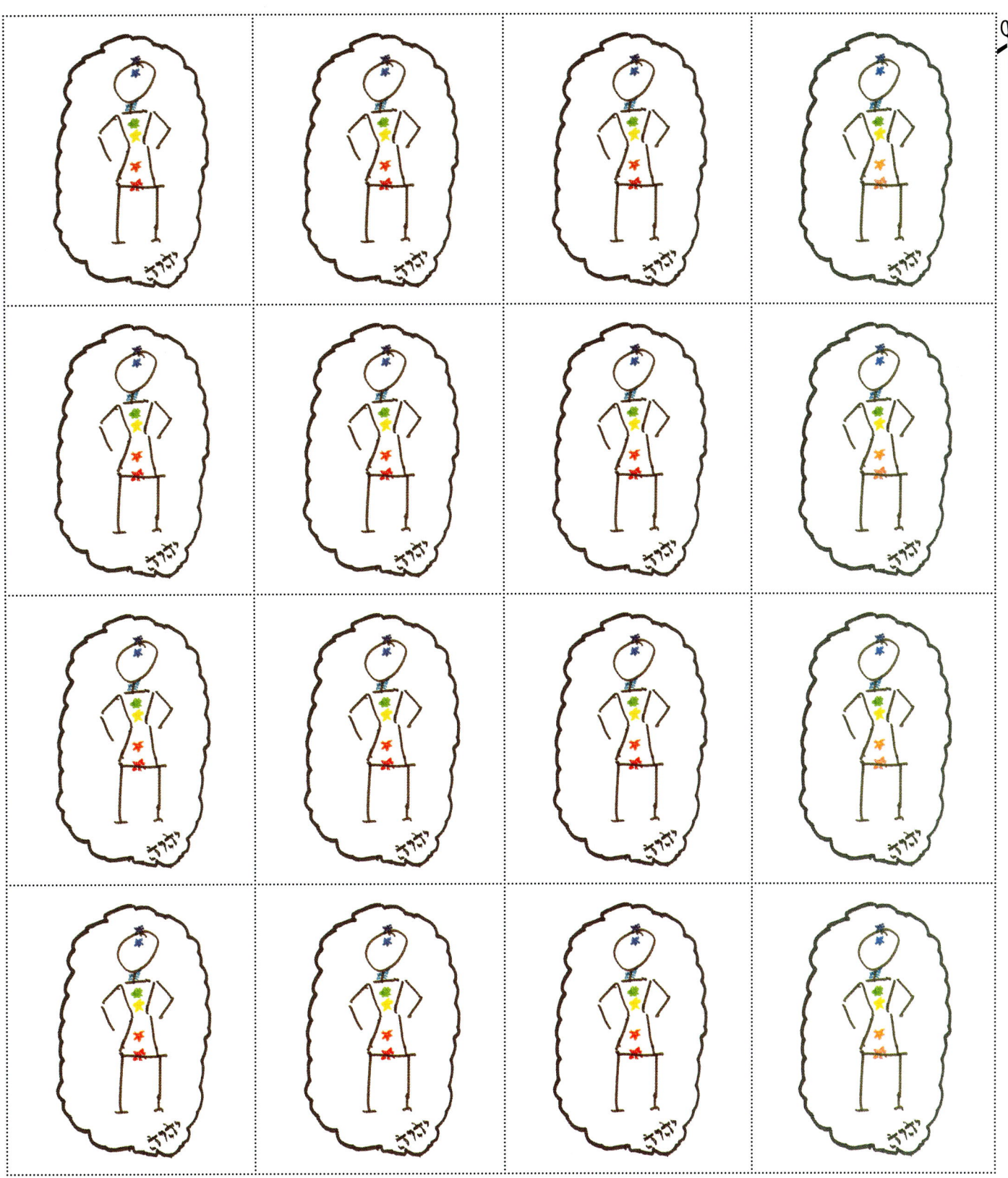

Suggested Affirmation: Creator, with Your help and guidance, I align all of my chakras, clear them of any afflictions and repair any disfigurement starting with my base chakra, moving up to my sacral chakra, my solar plexus, my heart chakra, my throat chakra, my third eye and my crown chakra. I see them restored to perfect balance. Thank You Creator for Your divine guidance and assistance.

Chakras

glyph **10**

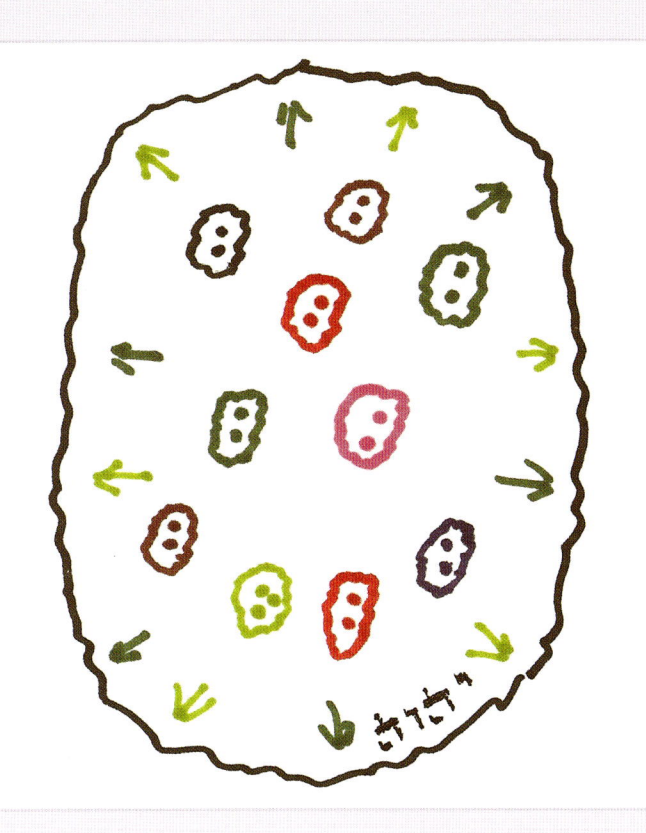

Anti-Bacterial Viral

For use on localized open wounds, place this glyph on top of the bandage. For use on an internal problem, place on the solar plexus, heart chakra, back of solar plexus, back of heart or any place that seems appropriate, preferably in blocks of four. For persistent conditions, the more glyphs the better. Leave on overnight. It is important to understand, however, that bacterial and viral illness are the result of a weakened immune system. When excess meat, sugar and other carbohydrates are consumed, the bodies pH balance is lowered, setting ourselves up for opportunistic invasions from bacteria, yeast and viruses. If a diet of fresh fruits and vegetables is followed, sickness will not be a problem. If pathogens have been invited in by poor eating habits, you must be willing to make some changes in your diet.

Suggested Affirmation: Creator, with Your loving help and guidance, I release to the Light all the pathogens that I now hold within me. I see myself as whole and well, full of Your love and Your Light, free of all disease.

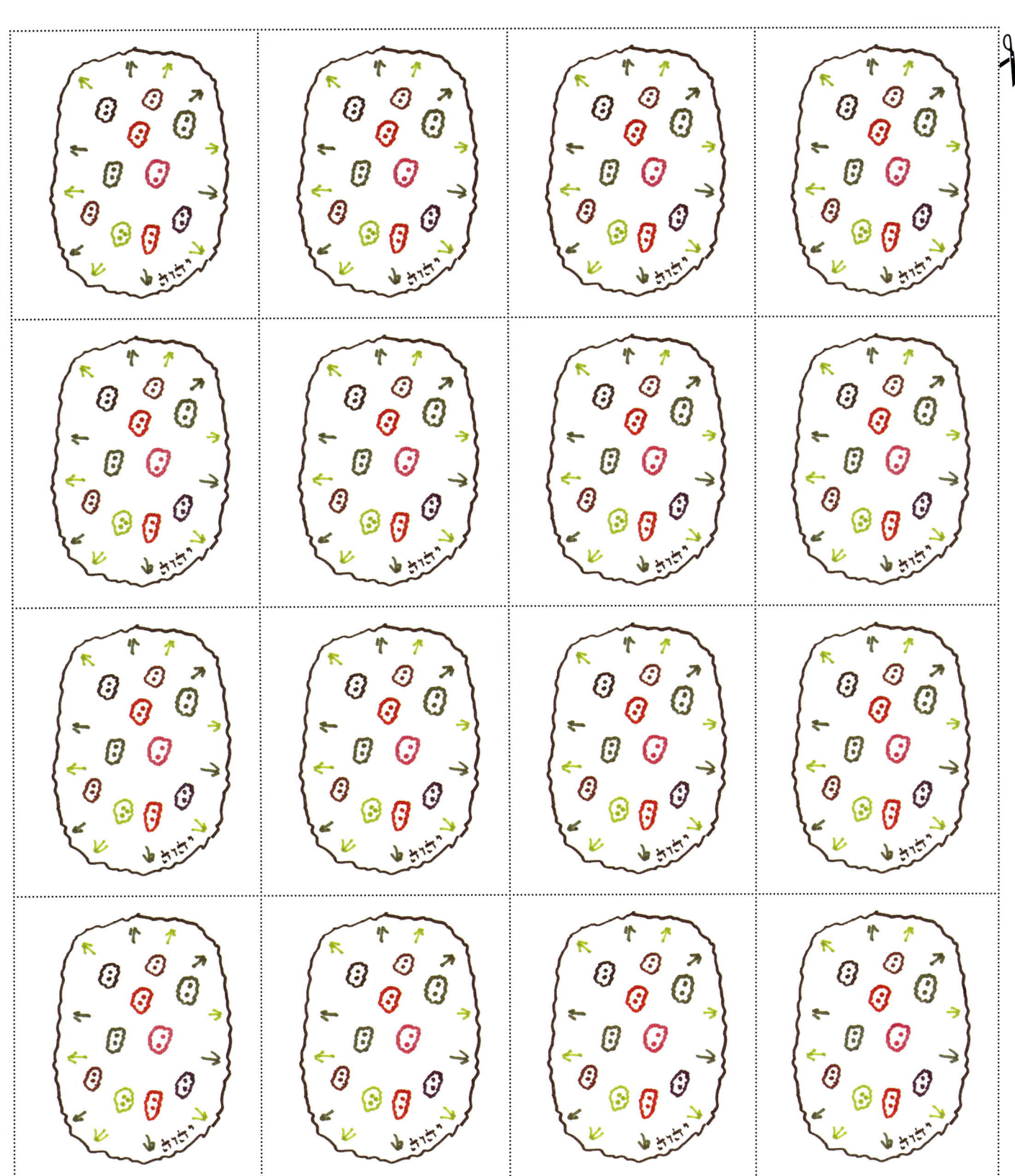

Suggested Affirmation: Creator, with Your loving help and guidance, I release to the Light all the pathogens that I now hold within me. I see myself as whole and well, full of Your love and Your Light, free of all disease.

Anti-Bacterial/Viral

glyph **13**

Grief Sadness Depression

This glyph can remove residual grief, sadness and depression from the body and aura. Place over the heart chakra, back of heart, any major chakra including the back, or the chakra governing the affected part. Depression always has underlying causes that must be understood and resolved.

Suggested Affirmation: I release all grief, sadness and depression that I have been holding within me. I replace these with joy and acceptance. I release all that is in my past and will live only in the now. I see myself as loving myself and others without judgement. I am grateful for all I have in my life.

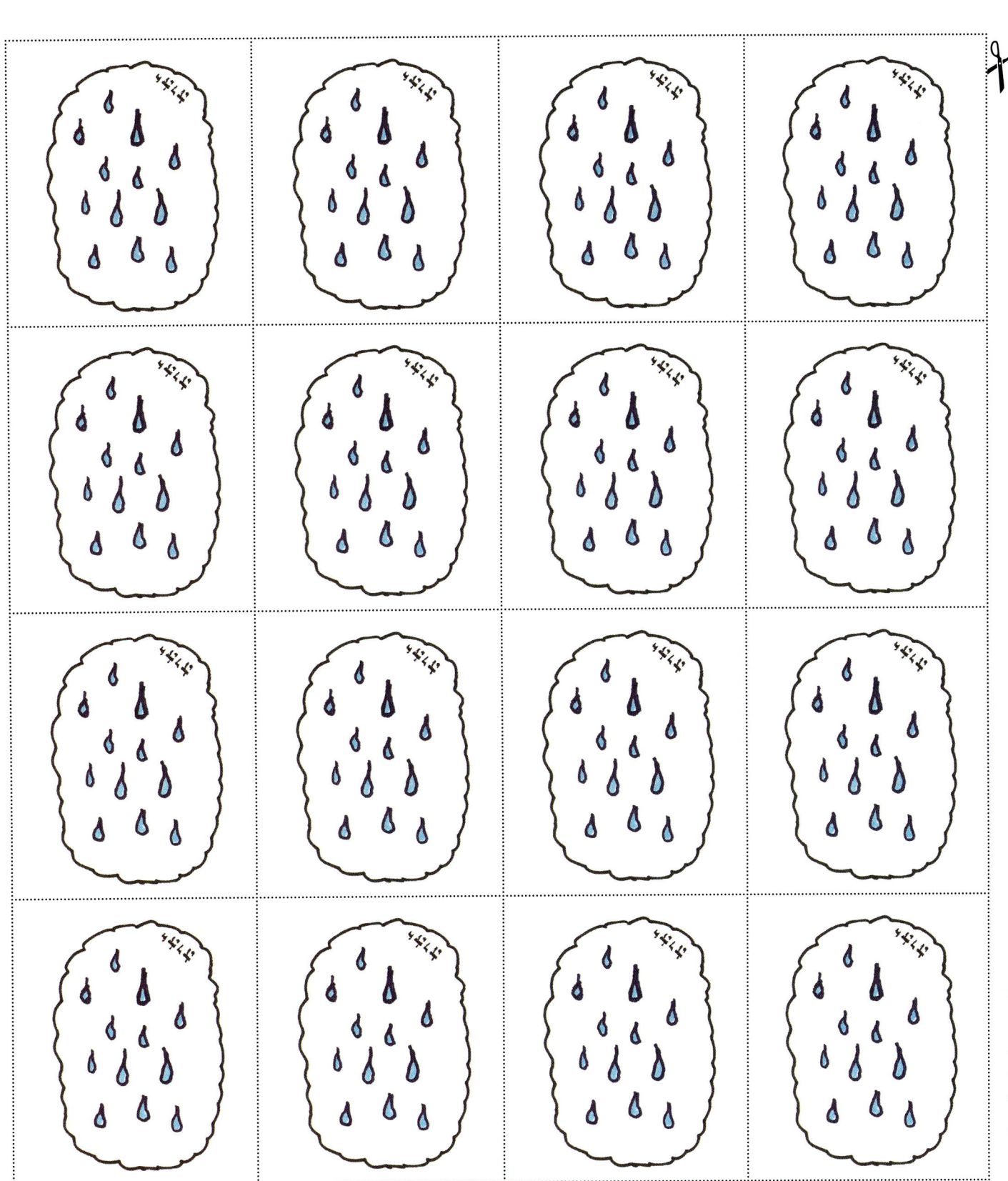

Suggested Affirmation: I release all grief, sadness and depression that I have been holding within me. I replace these with joy and acceptance. I release all that is in my past and will live only in the now. I see myself as loving myself and others without judgement. I am grateful for all I have in my life.

Grief – Sadness – Depression

glyph **14**

Relief from Tension and Anxiety

This glyph can send frequencies into the body that can aid in relaxation and promote inner harmony and balance. This glyph is also helpful when you have trouble falling asleep. Place on any major chakra or your navel. Empty your mind and practice deep breathing.

Suggested Affirmation: I release anything that is keeping me in a state of tension and stress. I relax myself and release all thoughts. I see myself in total control of my reality. Creator, thank You for helping me restore calm within my body.

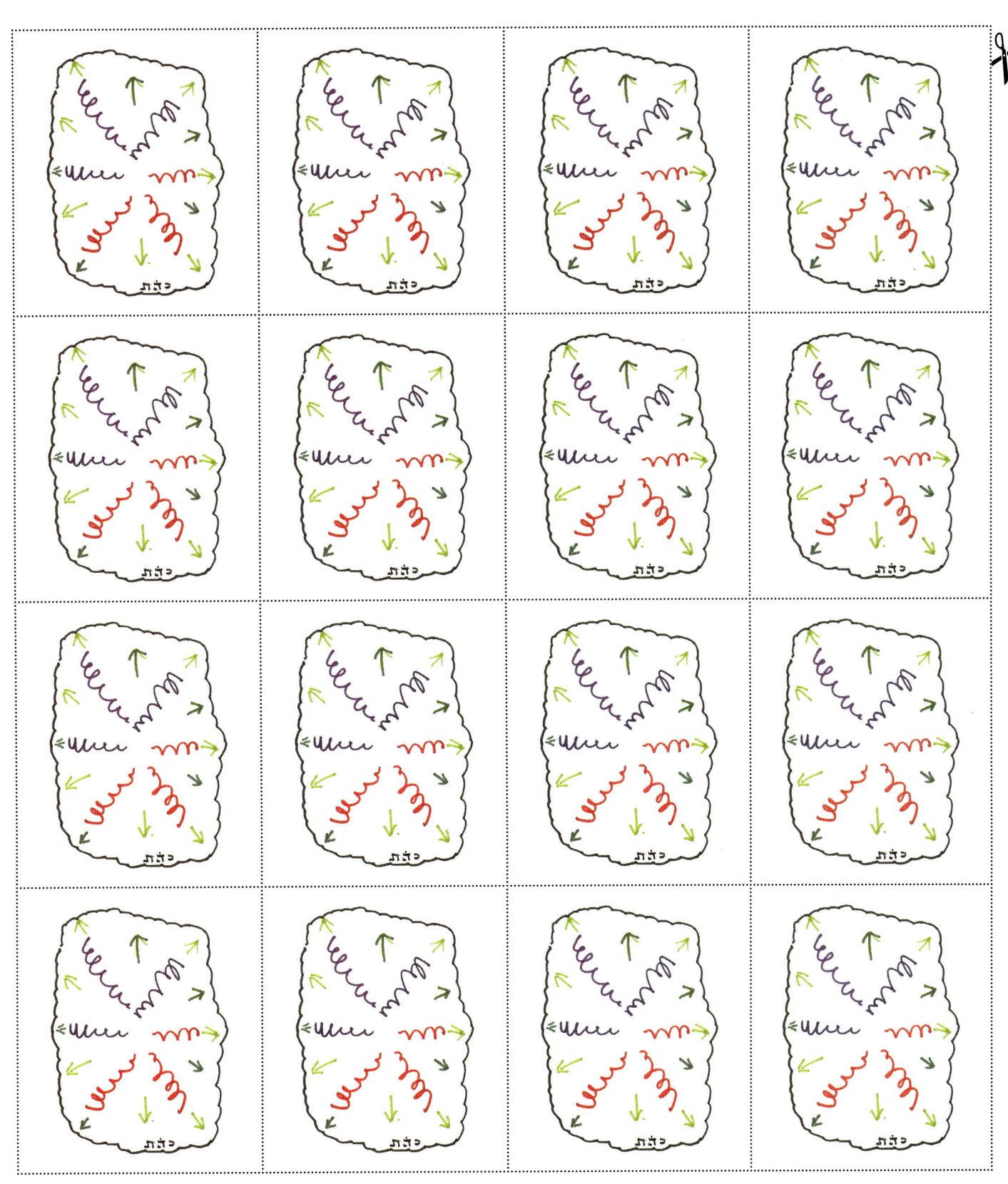

Suggested Affirmation: I release anything that is keeping me in a state of tension and stress. I relax myself and release all thoughts. I see myself in total control of my reality. Creator, thank You for helping me restore calm within my body.

Relief from Tension and Anxiety

glyph **15**

Parasites in Humans or Animals

For the removal of parasites on or in humans or animals, place this glyph in blocks of four on the solar plexus for the stomach and any other major chakra, organ or gland. For the liver, place a row or double row of these glyphs under the rib cage on the right side and wear overnight. For the spleen, place a row or double row of these glyphs over the spleen chakra under the left rib cage and leave on overnight. For the intestines or colon, place on the navel overnight. For skin parasites, place directly over affected area.

Suggested Affirmation: God, I let go of anything that is bugging me. I recognize that I can only achieve peace by trusting in You. I accept that I create my reality and that I am responsible for anything that I have attracted into my life. I ask for Your guidance. Thank You Creator.

Suggested Affirmation: God, I let go of anything that is bugging me. I recognize that I can only achieve peace by trusting in You. I accept that I create my reality and that I am responsible for anything that I have attracted into my life. I ask for Your guidance. Thank You Creator.

Parasites in Humans or Animals

glyph **16**

Release Vows

This glyph helps the user resolve any problems, situations or limitations that are affecting them in their present life, by releasing vows or contracts that they have made in a past life. Place this glyph on the solar plexus or the navel.

Suggested Affirmation: I release any and all vows that I may have made in my past that do not serve me in my present life. My body and mind are free of any bondage, able to move forward and be all that I am meant to be.

Suggested Affirmation: I release any and all vows that I may have made in my past that do not serve me in my present life. My body and mind are free of any bondage, able to move forward and be all that I am meant to be.

glyph **17**

Focus and Organization

When your life seems to be in confusion, you may be feeling scattered, and continually starting projects you never finish. This glyph can help you focus. Combined with your intention to organize your life, it can give you that little boost that you need. Place one over your solar plexus, your third eye, or any place you feel guided to put it.

Suggested Affirmation: God, help me to achieve order and balance in my life and overcome negative tendencies that are holding me back. I place my trust in the Creator. I intend Divine Light, guidance, and protection as I go throughout each and every day. Thank You God for the guidance I receive.

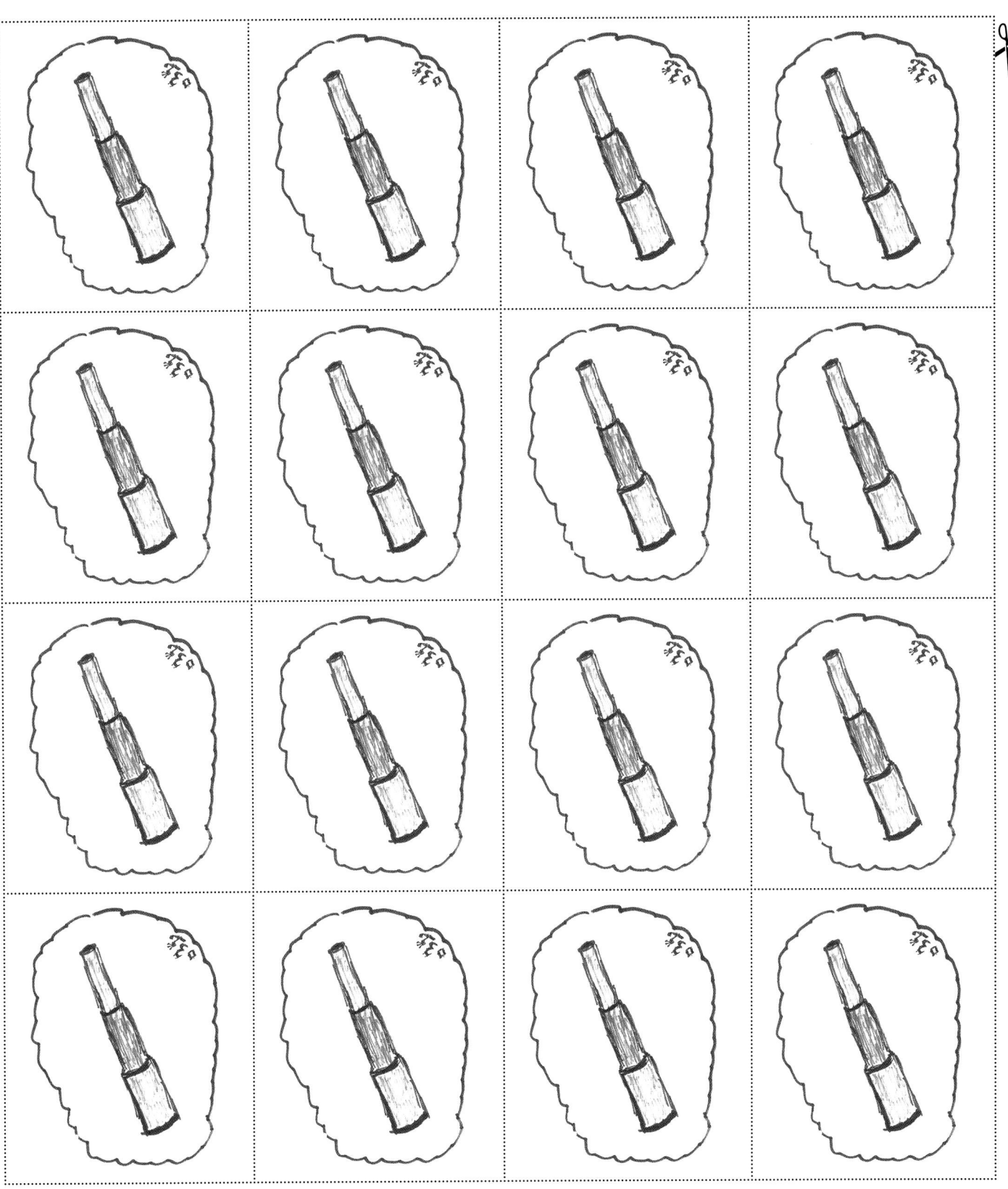

Suggested Affirmation: God, help me to achieve order and balance in my life and overcome negative tendencies that are holding me back. I place my trust in the Creator. I intend Divine Light, guidance, and protection as I go throughout each and every day. Thank You God for the guidance I receive.

75 Focus and Organization

glyph **18**

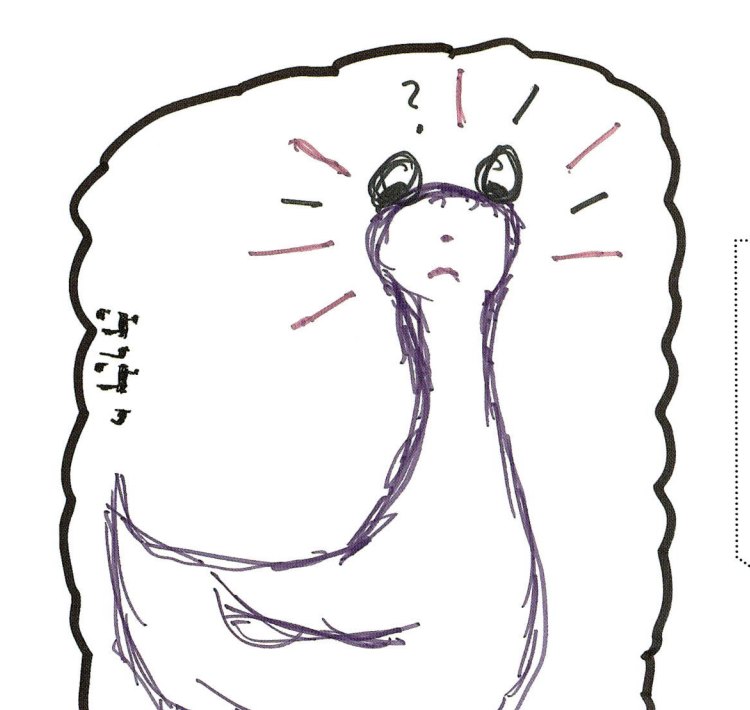

Heartache Fear of Abandonment

This glyph can give great relief from the fear of abandonment. It can also help heal the spiritual cord that can be torn due to the loss of a loved one regardless of the cause. Place it over the solar plexus or heart chakra. If the fear of abandonment is causing digestive distress, place the glyph on the navel.

Suggested Affirmation: Creator, I release all fear of being abandoned. I know You are my Source and will always be with me. Assist me in finding my purpose and moving forward in my life.

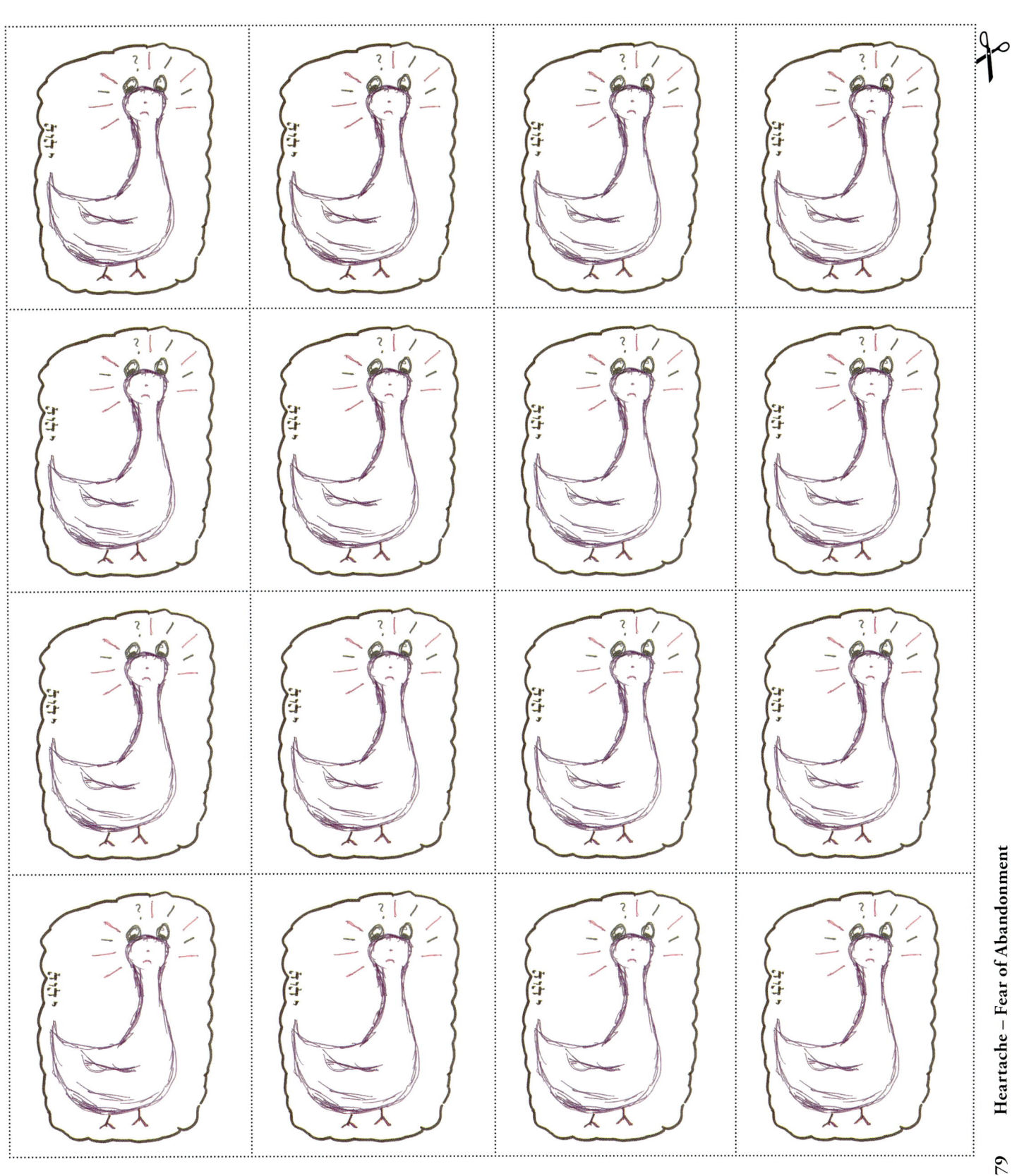

Suggested Affirmation: Creator, I release all fear of being abandoned. I know You are my Source and will always be with me. Assist me in finding my purpose and moving forward in my life.

glyph **19**

Bites from Insects

This glyph can neutralize the stinging from insect bites. Place over bite as soon as possible. For chiggers, use Glyph 15, Parasites, under this glyph to kill the insect. In the case of a life-threatening incident, seek prompt medical attention.

Suggested Affirmation: I know I am an extension of Source Energy and I am ready to release what is bothering me. I no longer see the irritants and see only the good. Thank You Creator for all the blessings and assistance that I receive.

Suggested Affirmation: I know I am an extension of Source Energy and I am ready to release what is bothering me. I no longer see the irritants and see only the good. Thank You Creator for all the blessings and assistance that I receive.

Bites from Insects

glyph **23**

Repair Damaged Nerves

This glyph can repair damaged nerve bundles. It is important to use this glyph only while you are lying down before bedtime as it may make you a little dizzy. The feeling will be gone after a short while. This glyph should be used on the third eye and crown chakra. It can also be used on the solar plexus or any other major chakra.

Suggested Affirmation: I let go of any and all afflictions that have been bothering me in the past. I see myself as healed. I am free and unencumbered. Life is good and I am in joy.

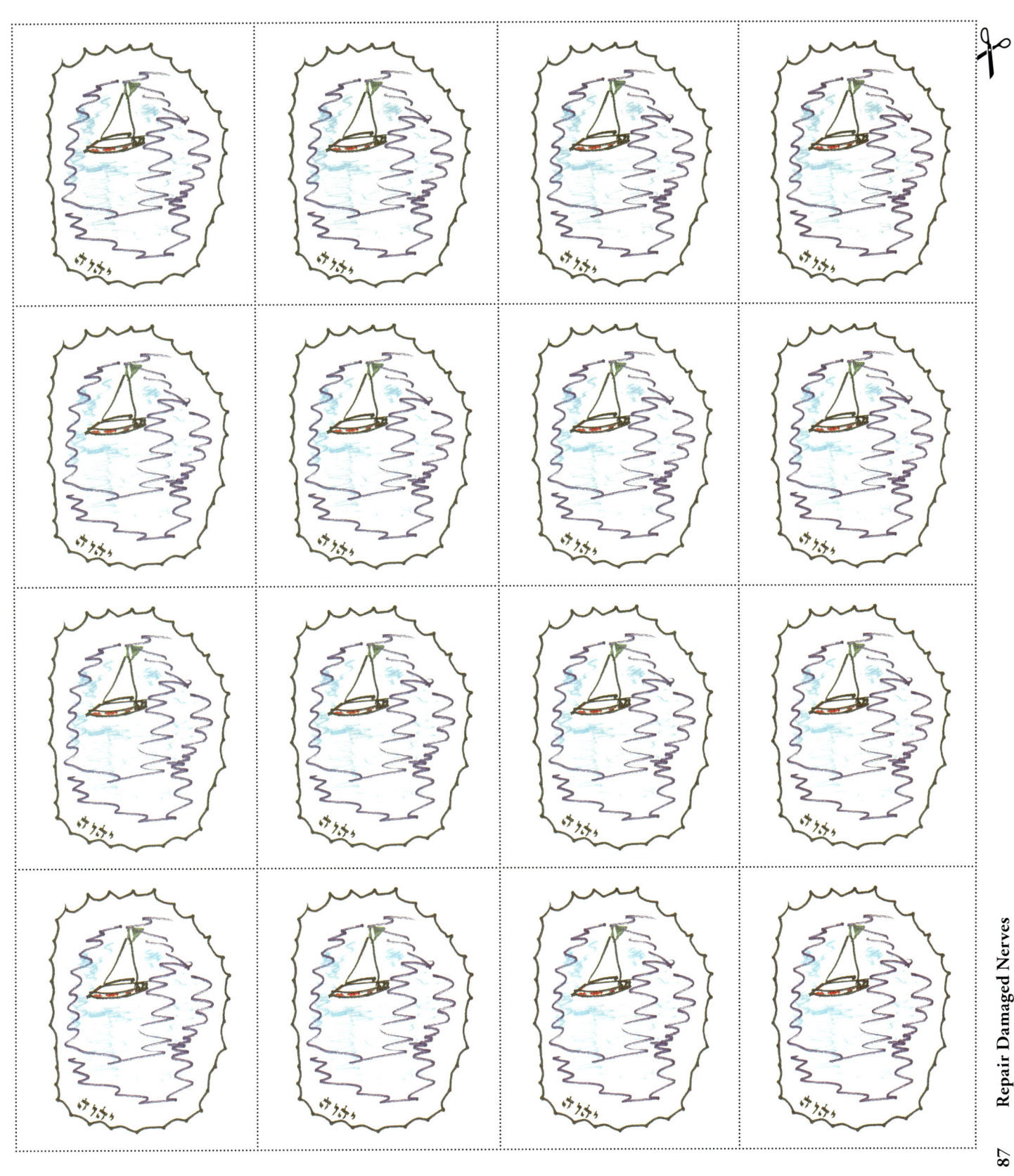

Suggested Affirmation: I let go of any and all afflictions that have been bothering me in the past. I see myself as healed. I am free and unencumbered. Life is good and I am in joy.

Repair Damaged Nerves

glyph **25**

Headaches
Energy Release

This glyph can relieve congestion in the nasal and forehead area caused by electronic devices, allergies or colds. Place the glyph on the ajna chakra and/or the third eye. Keep in mind that allergies and colds are the result of a weakened immune system and will disappear when the immune system is strengthened or by raising the pH balance.

Suggested Affirmation: I release whatever is causing me any stress in my life. I relax and let go. Creator, help me to understand how to let go and allow spirit to lead me.

Suggested Affirmation: I release whatever is causing me any stress in my life. I relax and let go. Creator, help me to understand how to let go and allow spirit to lead me.

Headaches – Energy Release

glyph **26**

Course Correct and Alignment

This glyph is to correct the neurologic function, perceptual center, nervous system and genetic stabilization. It can also align the body with celestial encounterments (planets or other celestial objects). Place this glyph on the crown chakra, third eye, the solar plexus or anywhere that feels appropriate.

Suggested Affirmation: Creator, with Your loving guidance, I place myself in harmony with my chosen mission and move forward with courage. I align my mind and body with the universe. May I stay forever on the path of love.

Suggested Affirmation: Creator, with Your loving guidance, I place myself in harmony with my chosen mission and move forward with courage. I align my mind and body with the universe. May I stay forever on the path of love.

glyph **29**

Abundance Gene Activation Reconnect DNA

Use this glyph for assistance in activating your abundance gene and removing blocks to abundance. This glyph will be helpful, but you must understand that you create your abundance with your mind. If you see yourself as abundant, you will be abundant. If you see yourself as struggling, or in a state of poverty and lack, you will continue to find yourself in that position. If you fear the problems or results of poverty, that fear will draw to you what you fear. The abundance gene can only help you if you are willing to let go of these negative patterns. Place this glyph on all major chakras, back of chakras or any place you might be holding fear of poverty or past life associations with poverty.

Suggested Affirmation: Creator, I see myself as flowing with Your abundance. Thank You God for all that I have received and continue to receive.

Suggested Affirmation: Creator, I see myself as flowing with Your abundance. Thank You God for all that I have received and continue to receive.

glyph **30**

General Balancing

The purpose of this glyph is to balance the Spheno-Basilar junction in the brain, balance the cortices, provide body switching when needed, and activate body hydration balancing. This glyph should be placed on the third eye or anywhere you feel guided to use it. Use often.

Suggested Affirmation: I see myself in total balance. With the power of God within me, I maintain perfect balance and coordination. I keep love in my heart for myself and others.

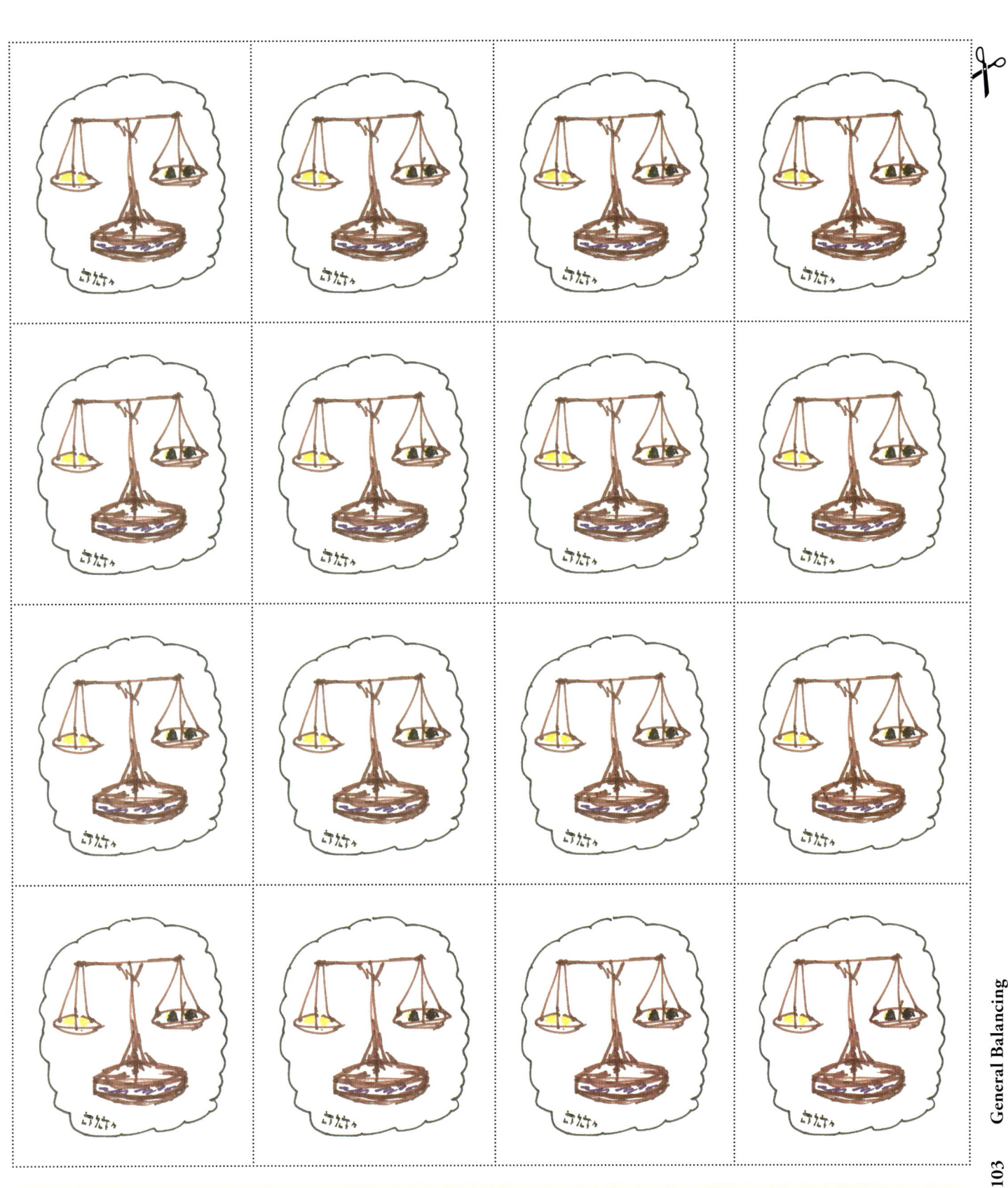

Suggested Affirmation: I see myself in total balance. With the power of God within me, I maintain perfect balance and coordination. I keep love in my heart for myself and others.

glyph **46**

Love Frequency

The purpose of this glyph is to program all receptors in the body to the frequency of love. This glyph can produce amazing results when placed on the heart chakra during times of stress or anger. It can be used on the solar plexus or any other chakra. This glyph can also be placed on a picture or even the name of a friend or loved one, to help them in stressful times.

Suggested Affirmation: Creator, I hold only love in my heart. I release everything from within me that is not love. As I see others, I see only the good in them and let go of anything else. I am grateful for all things.

Suggested Affirmation: Creator, I hold only love in my heart. I release everything from within me that is not love. As I see others, I see only the good in them and let go of anything else. I am grateful for all things.

glyph **50**

Reaching Out

This glyph can help raise the consciousness of individuals or animals not physically present. All of the information from glyphs that are intended to remove negative emotions and resolve dysfunction, will be pulsed to the individual of choice, one glyph each day. Place this glyph face down on top of a picture or the name of a family member, loved one, or any other person that you desire this positive energy to be sent. This produces a very subtle effect so improvement will come slowly. This glyph is programmed to continue for six weeks. If more assistance is desired, instruct the glyph to start the program again.

Suggested Affirmation: Creator, I ask that the energy of all of these glyphs be sent out to help others. I see these people receiving the healing energy. I know there is no limit to the power of this prayerful intent.

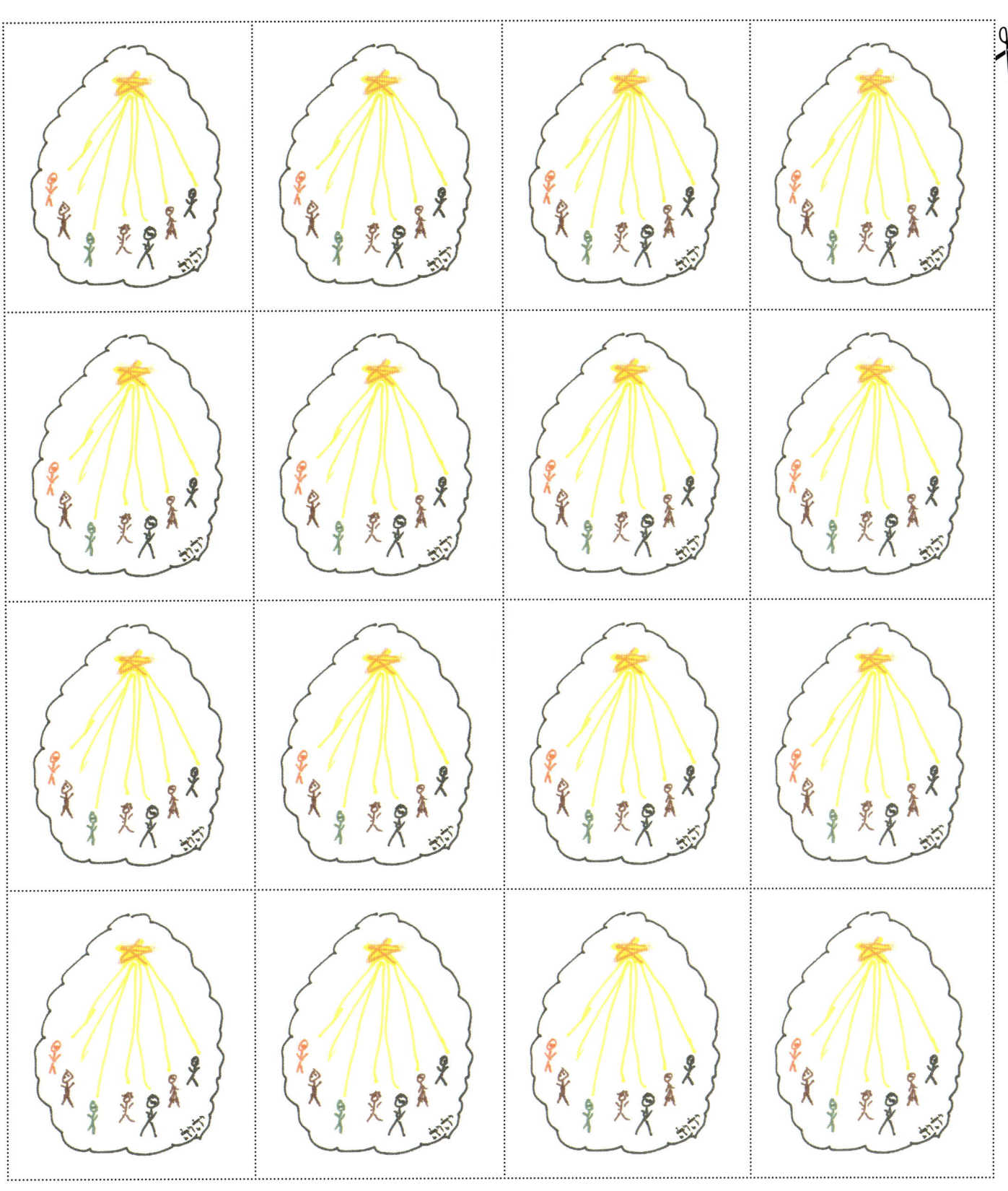

Suggested Affirmation: Creator, I ask that the energy of all of these glyphs be sent out to help others. I see these people receiving the healing energy. I know there is no limit to the power of this prayerful intent.

Reaching Out

glyph **52**

People of the World

The message of this glyph is to send all of the people of the world the energy of love and hope, to help deliver them from bondage, and pulse the earth with peace. Wear this glyph over your heart chakra to send the following message to the world. "Pulse all of the people of the world with (the frequency of) love, forgiveness, and absence of fear. Reach out to all who are in need and touch them with hope. Reach out and deliver all beings from bondage to others who would use them for their gain. Pulse the earth with (the frequency of) peace and love until it is full."

Suggested Affirmation: Pulse all of the people of the world with the frequency of love, forgiveness, and absence of fear. Reach out to all who are in need and touch them with hope. Reach out and deliver all beings from bondage to others who would use them for their gain. Pulse the earth with peace and love until it is full.

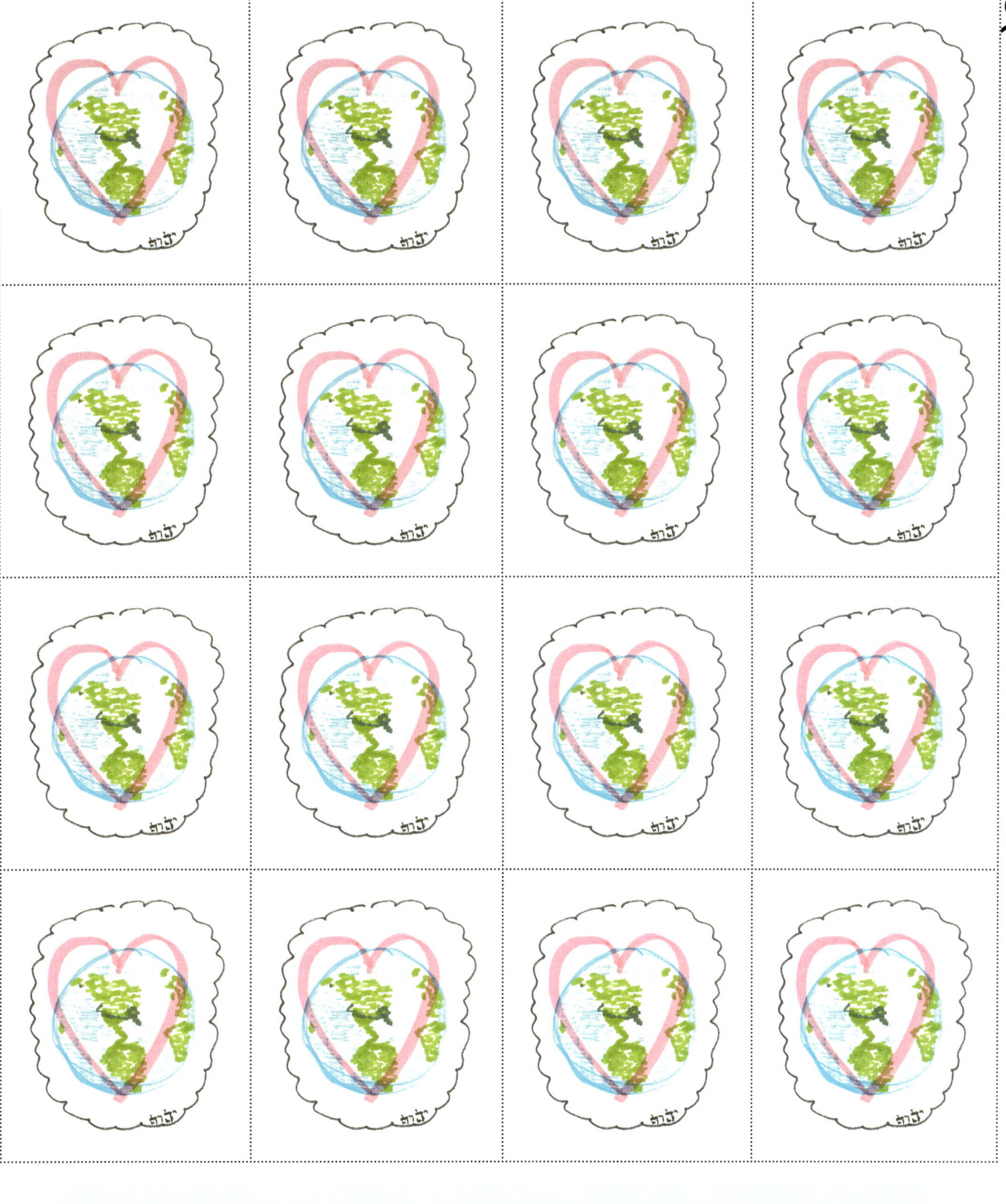

Suggested Affirmation: Pulse all of the people of the world with the frequency of love, forgiveness, and absence of fear. Reach out to all who are in need and touch them with hope. Reach out and deliver all beings from bondage to others who would use them for their gain. Pulse the earth with peace and love until it is full.

People of the World

glyph **55**

Sever Agreements of Pain

This glyph can sever an agreement of pain and suffering between the members who have made the agreement and the user of the glyph. Sometimes in past lives, where suffering was great, people made an agreement that they would all suffer together. In subsequent lives, this agreement may have a negative impact on the people concerned. This glyph is designed to break that agreement to allow one to be free of any bondage. Place this glyph on the solar plexus, navel, or any other chakra or place that seems to be indicated.

Suggested Affirmation: I separate myself from any participation in any agreement of pain and suffering. I release any others from any like agreement that may have included me. I pray for their highest good.

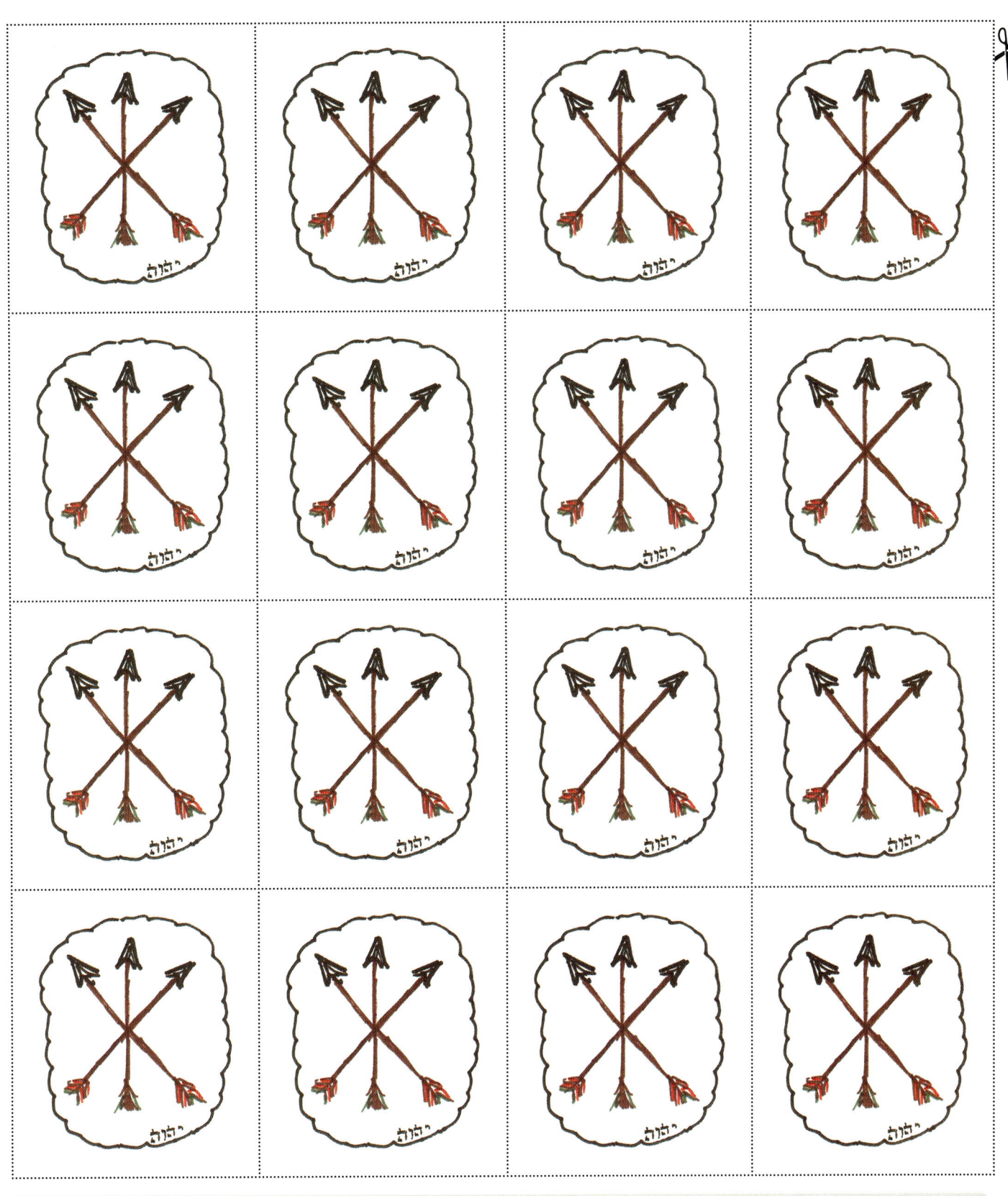

Suggested Affirmation: I separate myself from any participation in any agreement of pain and suffering. I release any others from any like agreement that may have included me. I pray for their highest good.

Sever Agreements of Pain

glyph **56**

Clearing Energy

The purpose of this glyph is to work toward removing the blocks to help us understand who we are and why we are here. This glyph, plus prayer and meditation, can help remove much of what is holding us back and keeping us from understanding our mission. Place on the solar plexus and all major chakras, including the back, as well as minor chakras and any other place you feel guided to do so. You cannot use this glyph too often. We all hold a lot of "stuff" so do not expect too much, too soon.

Suggested Affirmation: I release anything that is keeping me from remembering who I am and why I am here. I release anything that is blocking me from remembering what I need to know to fulfill my mission in this lifetime. Thank You God for all of Your Light and assistance.

Suggested Affirmation: I release anything that is keeping me from remembering who I am and why I am here. I release anything that is blocking me from remembering what I need to know to fulfill my mission in this lifetime. Thank You God for all of Your Light and assistance.

glyph **61**

Remove Attached Entities

This glyph can remove any attached entities or demons, provided the affirmation is said with deliberation and intent when using it. Place on solar plexus, navel or wherever you feel guided to use it.

Suggested Affirmation: I order the expulsion of any demons or other dimensional beings from within or about my body or aura that are not present for my highest good. I instruct Archangel Michael and his legion of protectors to gather up and carry these beings over the veil and seal the portal against their return. I extend my gratitude for this service. I invoke a protective shield around myself and my aura to prevent the attachment of any negative energy. I hold myself in love and joy to avoid attracting any energy that is not of Light.

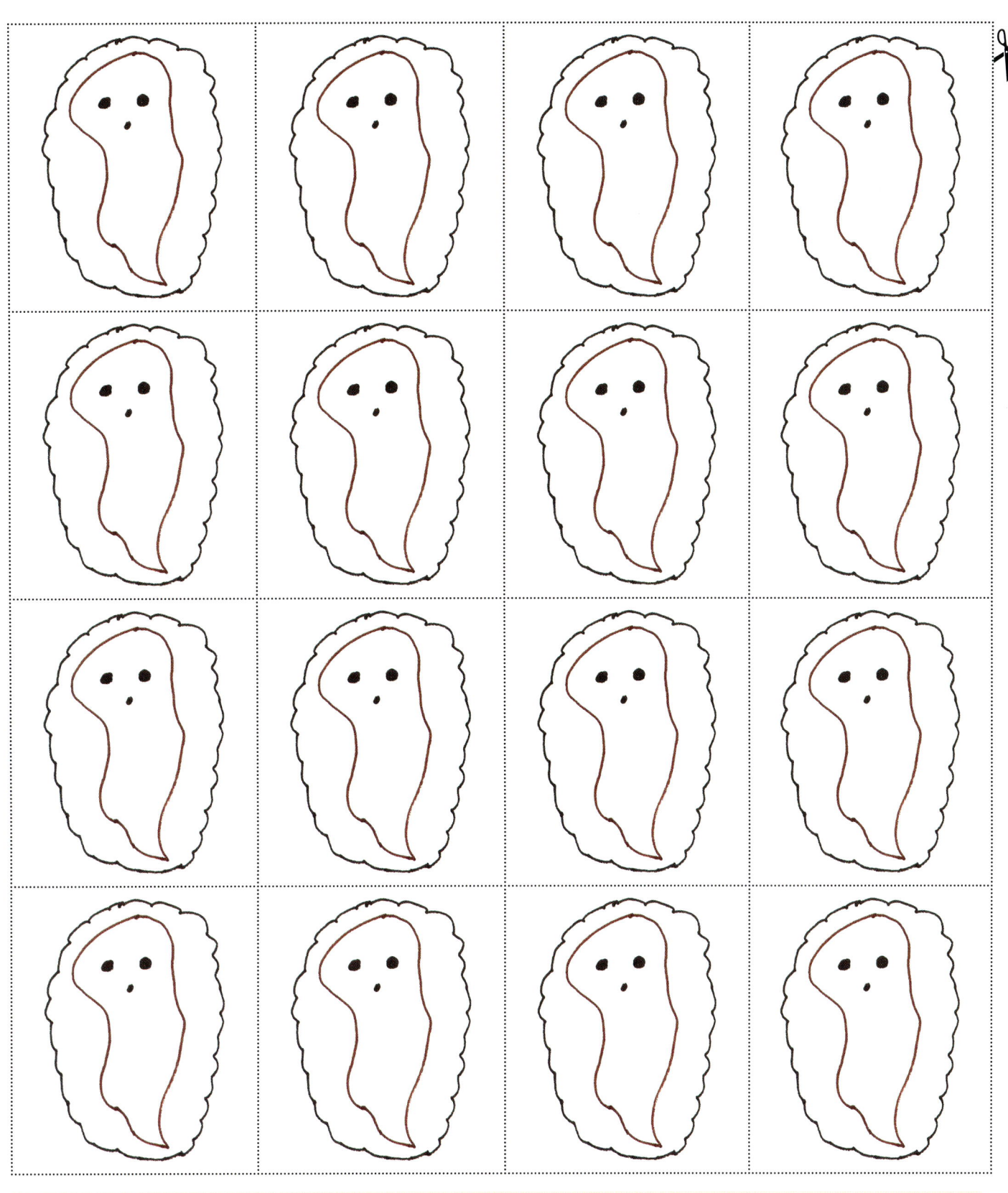

Suggested Affirmation: I order the expulsion of any demons or other dimensional beings from within or about my body or aura that are not present for my highest good. I instruct Archangel Michael and his legion of protectors to gather up and carry these beings over the veil and seal the portal against their return. I extend my gratitude for this service. I invoke a protective shield around myself and my aura to prevent the attachment of any negative energy. I hold myself in love and joy to avoid attracting any energy that is not of Light.

glyph **73**

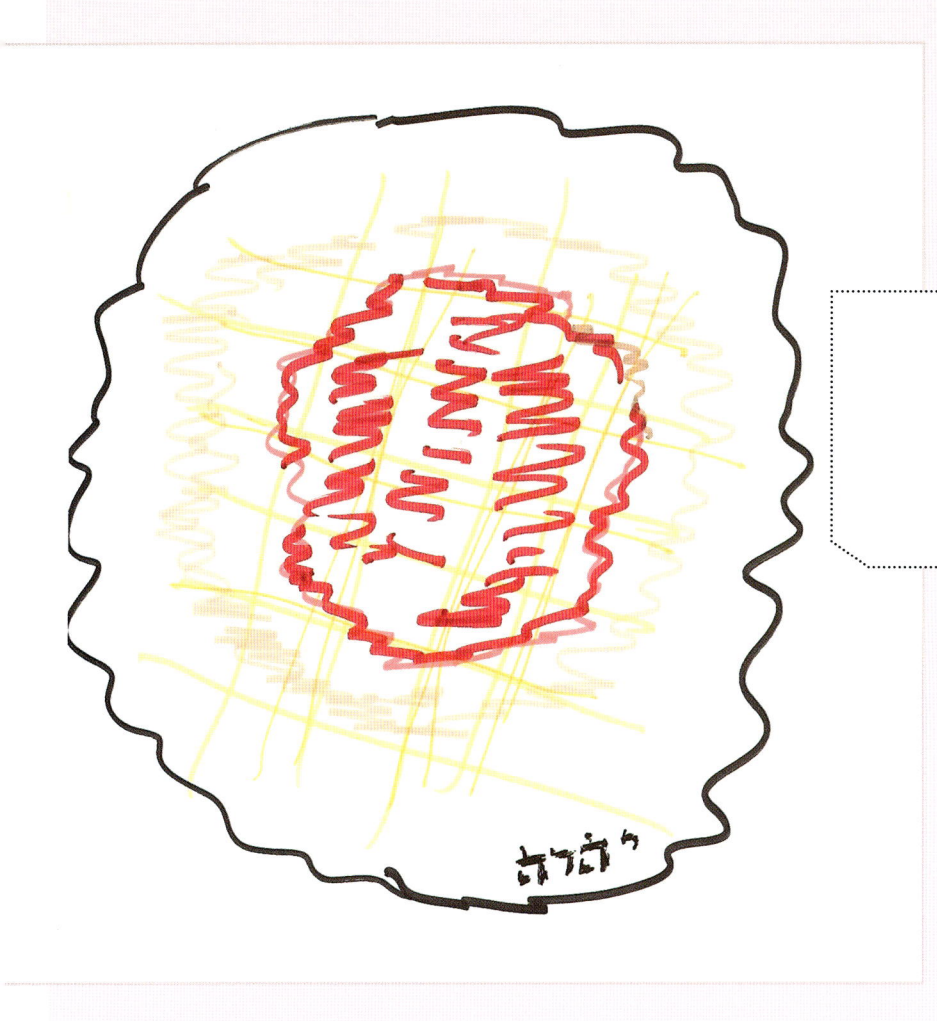

Cellular Repair

This glyph can bring about the rapid healing of all types of wounds including cuts, abrasions or torn skin. It can also speed up the healing of injured ligaments, cartilage, tendons and broken bones. Do not use on broken bones until after being set by a qualified medical practitioner.

Suggested Affirmation: Creator, using Your power that lies within me, I energize myself to rapidly heal the affliction from which I suffer. I honor You and express my gratitude for what I have learned from this. I heal myself now, with Your love and creative power.

Suggested Affirmation: Creator, using Your power that lies within me, I energize myself to rapidly heal the affliction from which I suffer. I honor You and express my gratitude for what I have learned from this. I heal myself now, with Your love and creative power.

Cellular Repair

glyph 82

Courage, Confidence and Joy

The purpose of this prayer glyph is to replace fear with the frequencies of courage, self-confidence and other positive attributes. Place this glyph on the heart chakra, solar plexus, or any major chakra including the back.

Suggested Affirmation: Creator, help me to release all the fear that is holding me back. I am grateful for all that You share with me. As You have given me the power to create, I do only that which is of the highest good.

Suggested Affirmation: Creator, help me to release all the fear that is holding me back. I am grateful for all that You share with me. As You have given me the power to create, I do only that which is of the highest good.

Appendix A: Glyph Chart

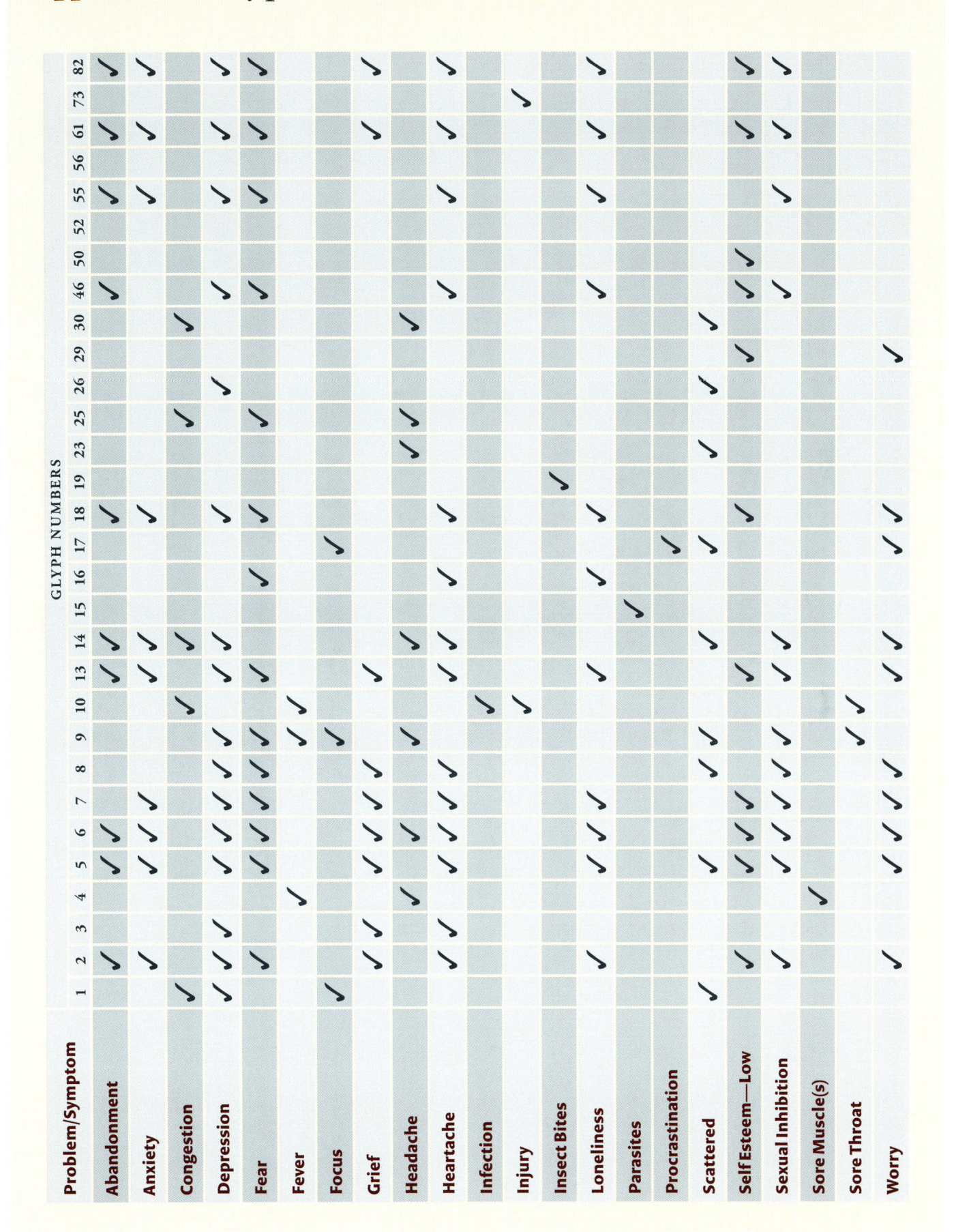

Problem/Symptom	1	2	3	4	5	6	7	8	9	10	13	14	15	16	17	18	19	23	25	26	29	30	46	50	52	55	56	61	73	82
Abandonment		♪			♪	♪					♪	♪				♪							♪			♪		♪		♪
Anxiety		♪			♪		♪				♪	♪				♪														
Congestion	♪	♪								♪		♪								♪		♪				♪		♪		♪
Depression		♪	♪		♪	♪	♪		♪		♪	♪							♪				♪					♪		♪
Fear			♪		♪	♪	♪		♪			♪		♪		♪			♪				♪			♪		♪		♪
Fever				♪						♪																				
Focus	♪										♪				♪															♪
Grief		♪	♪		♪	♪	♪	♪				♪																		
Headache		♪			♪	♪	♪					♪							♪			♪						♪		
Heartache		♪	♪		♪	♪	♪	♪	♪					♪		♪							♪							
Infection										♪																				
Injury										♪																			♪	
Insect Bites						♪	♪								♪		♪													
Loneliness			♪			♪	♪		♪		♪	♪			♪								♪					♪		
Parasites																														
Procrastination																♪			♪											
Scattered	♪																				♪									
Self Esteem—Low		♪				♪	♪		♪		♪	♪				♪					♪		♪	♪				♪		♪
Sexual Inhibition		♪				♪	♪		♪			♪											♪	♪		♪		♪		♪
Sore Muscle(s)				♪																										
Sore Throat									♪	♪																				
Worry		♪			♪	♪	♪					♪				♪					♪									

GLYPH NUMBERS

137

Appendix B:
Locating the Chakras

These drawings are provided to help you locate the chakras. If you put your hand on top of your head you will feel a warm spot. (This may be more difficult to locate if you are bald.) There is a slightly warm spot at the location of each of the other chakras that is easier to notice through a bulky material. If you are still unsure that you have the right location, cut a group of four of the glyphs to insure coverage of the right chakra.

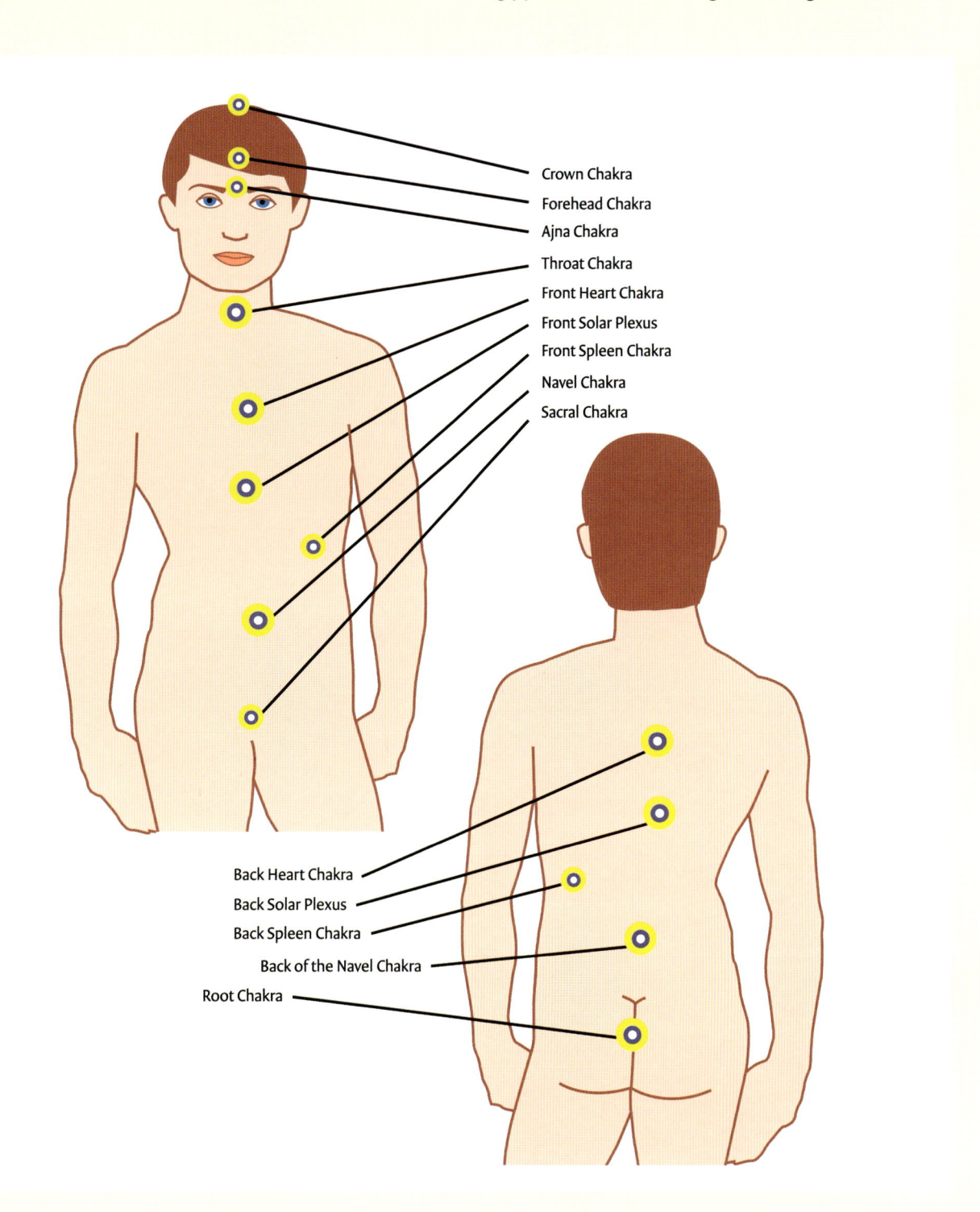

- Crown Chakra
- Forehead Chakra
- Ajna Chakra
- Throat Chakra
- Front Heart Chakra
- Front Solar Plexus
- Front Spleen Chakra
- Navel Chakra
- Sacral Chakra

- Back Heart Chakra
- Back Solar Plexus
- Back Spleen Chakra
- Back of the Navel Chakra
- Root Chakra

The chakras of an animal can also be located by a warm spot through their hair or fur. It is easier to locate and position a glyph on the back side of the animal. This should be done when they are sleeping. Dowsing Charts are provided in Appendix C to help you locate what glyphs you need and where to put them.

Instructions are also provided. This drawing of a dog is provided to show the location of the backside chakras. The front, or underside, will be directly opposite. The chakras on a cat are in the same location as they are on a dog. Concentrate on the pet or a picture of the pet when dowsing.

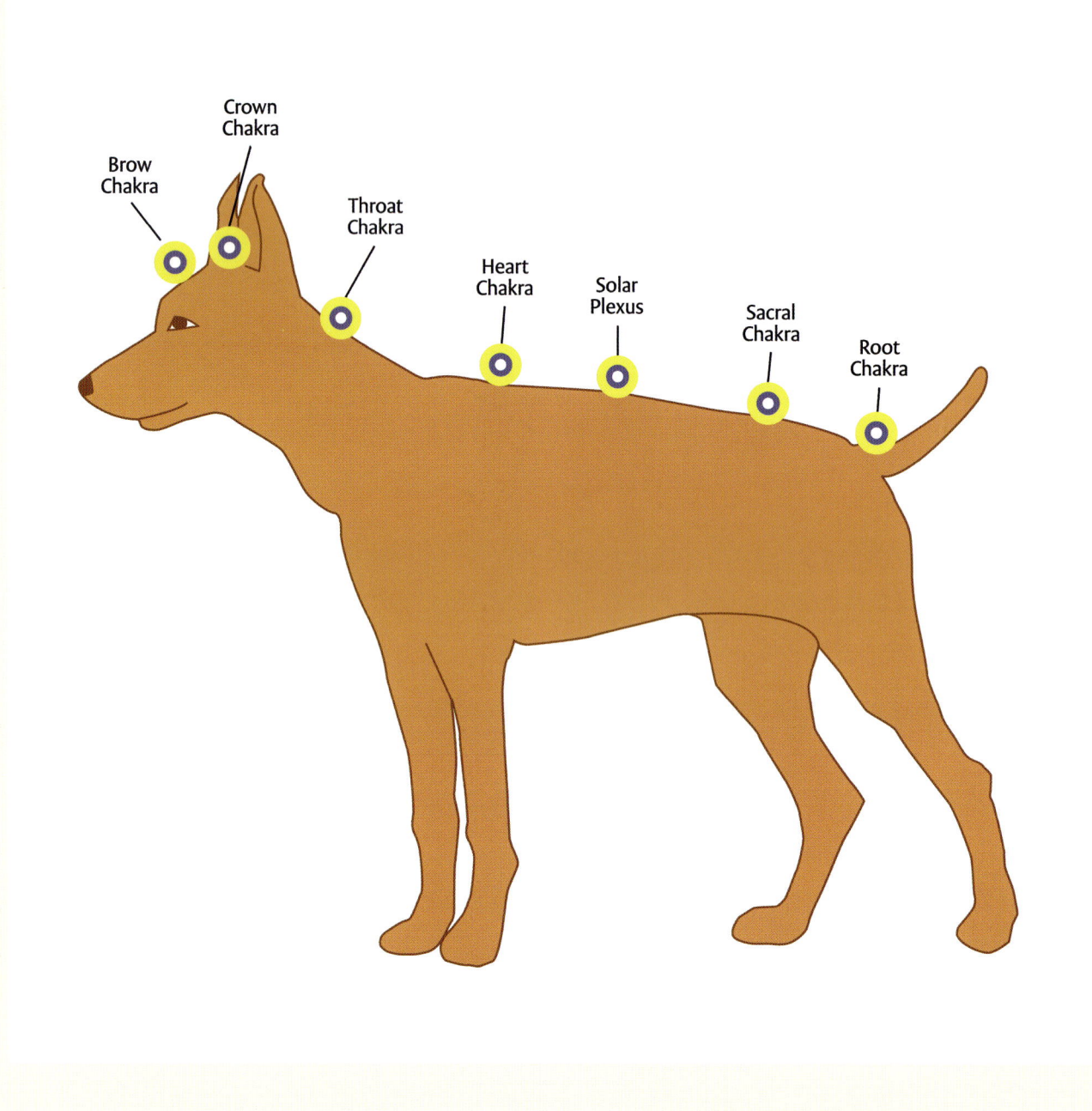

Appendix C:
Dowsing

An excellent method of finding out which glyph you need (or your pet needs) is through dowsing. This manual will state briefly how dowsing works, but for a thorough explanation, it is strongly recommended that you purchase the book, *Letter to Robin: A Mini Course in Pendulum Dowsing* by Walt Woods. The charts on the next page are designed to help you locate which glyphs are needed and where they should be placed on the body. Dowsing of this type is done with a pendulum, which can be purchased at any gem and crystal shop. A pendulum is a very useful tool that can provide you with answers to many questions. Once you have your pendulum, program it by telling it which direction you want it to swing for a yes answer, (usually back and forth in front of you) and what way it should swing for a no (side to side). Remember, you tell the pendulum, it does not tell you. It is important to clear your mind of any outcome or your own energy will cause the pendulum to swing in the direction your mind is telling it, rather than the universal energy that would give you the correct answer. A little practice will help you considerably. It does not matter if you make a mistake and select a glyph that is not needed, or put it on the wrong place. The worst that can happen is nothing. No harm can come from any of the glyphs. They are completely safe.

When selecting a pendulum, pick one that feels right to you. It does not matter what it is made of, but should have sufficient weight to have a good swing. Use the charts often since your needs will change as you continue to release more and more. The prayer glyphs are an easy, pain free method of releasing emotional burdens. They are a great deal safer than drugs. Little by little, you will feel lighter and more carefree as you shed layers of fear, guilt, shame, sadness and many other negative emotions that are holding you back and keeping you from being who you really are.

There are two charts for the glyph numbers. The first is for the glyph numbers 1-17 and the second one is for the numbers 18-82. The third chart is for the location on your body that you should place the glyph. After you have used your pendulum to locate the glyph you need, go right to the third chart to find out where you should place the glyph without looking to see what is the name or number. This will help prevent you from trying to guess where the glyph should go. You may be surprised at where the pendulum tells you to put the glyph. Remember, everything is connected.

Glyph Dowsing Chart #1

"Which glyph will I find most helpful right now?"

Glyph Dowsing Chart #2

"Which glyph will I find most helpful right now?"

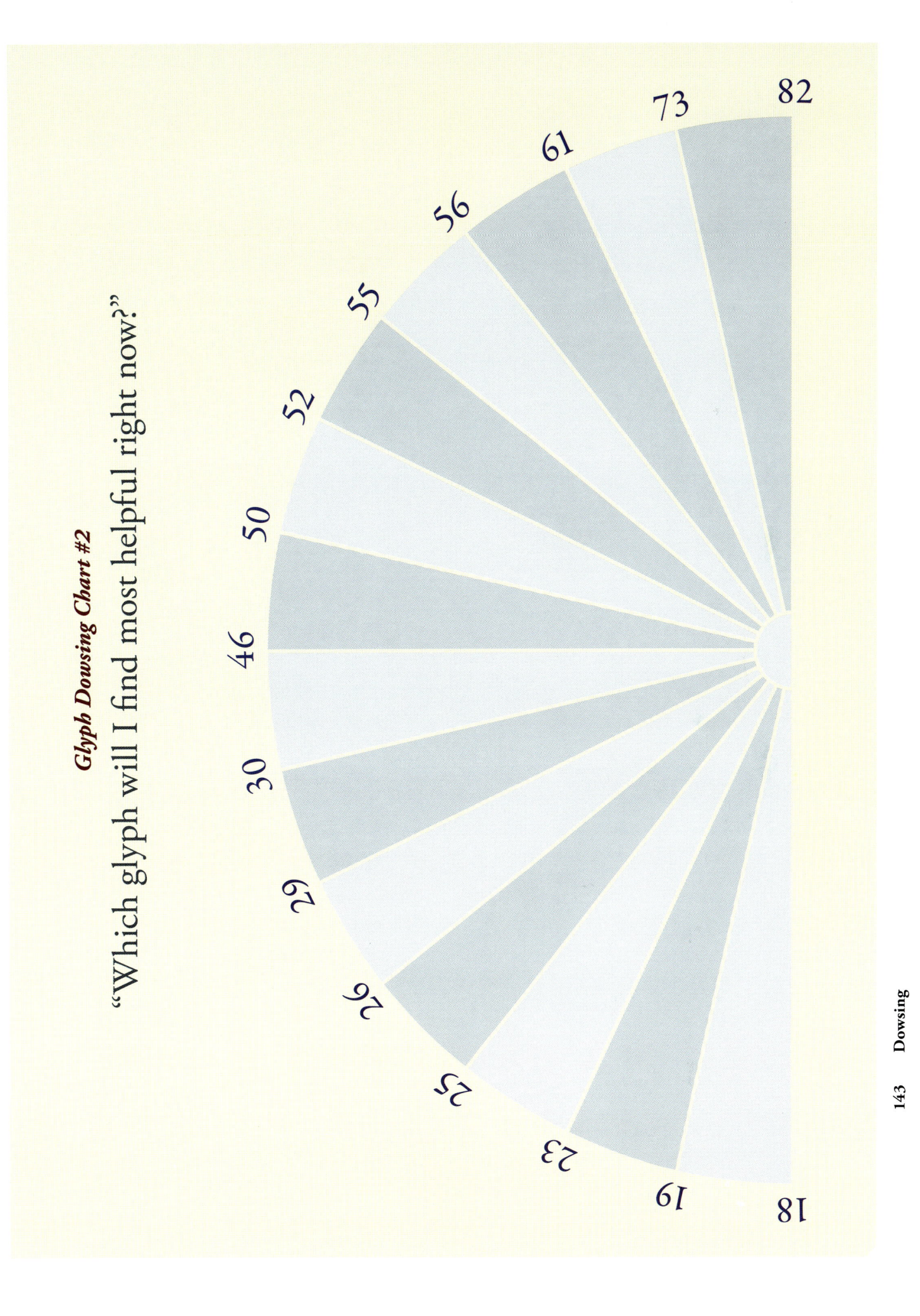

18 19 23 25 26 29 30 46 50 52 55 56 61 73 82

143   Dowsing

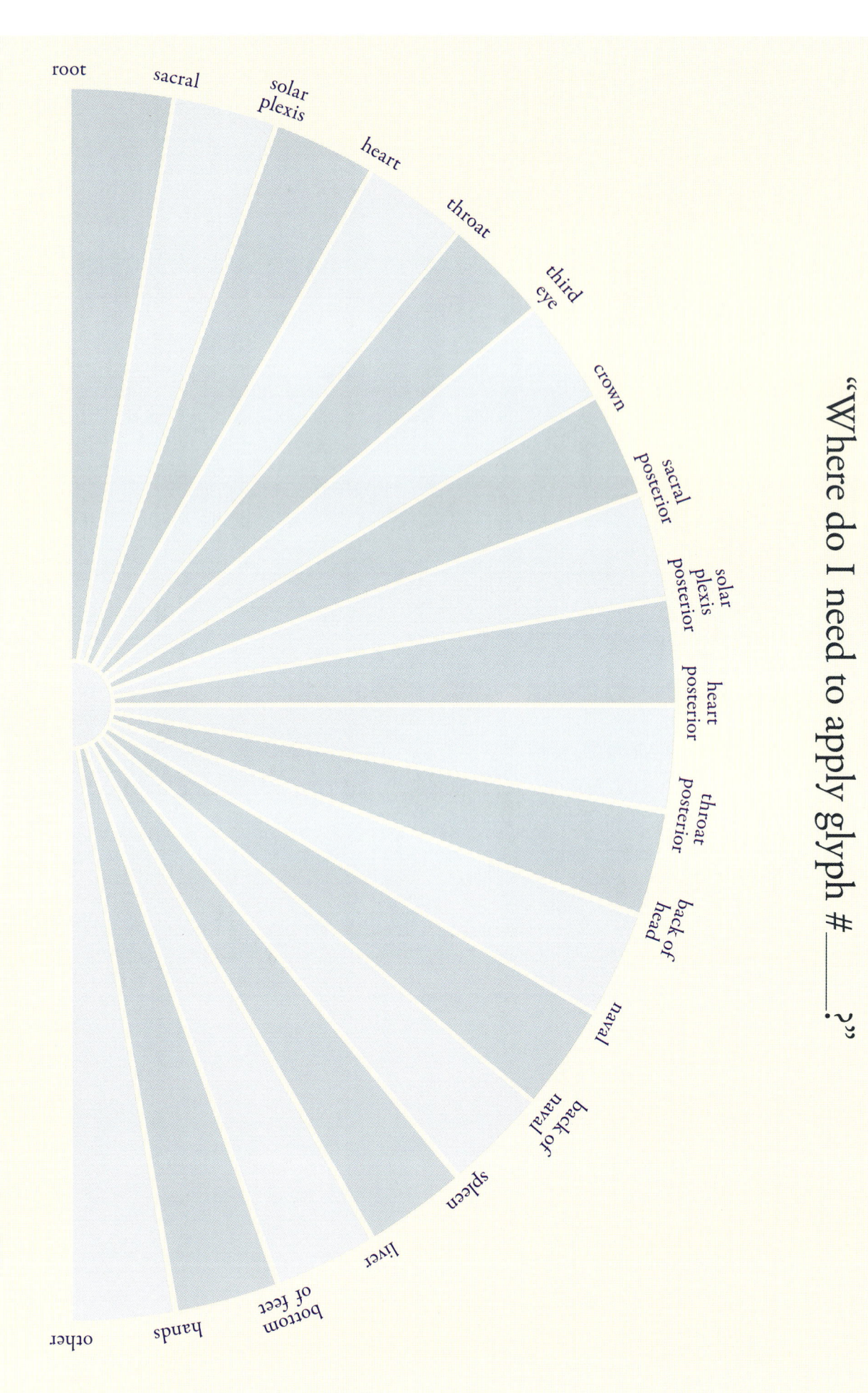

Glyph Dowsing Chart #3

"Where do I need to apply glyph #____?"

- root
- sacral
- solar plexis
- heart
- throat
- third eye
- crown
- sacral posterior
- solar plexis posterior
- heart posterior
- throat posterior
- back of head
- naval
- back of naval
- spleen
- liver
- bottom of feet
- hands
- other

Dowsing

Appendix D:
AcuTapping (Emotional Release Technique)

Acutapping, also know as Thought Field Therapy or Emotional Release Technique, is another powerful way to remove negative emotions when they are in our present thoughts. By tapping with our fingers on various acupuncture points, we can release these negative emotions easily and quickly. Memorize the Basic Tapping Sequence below. Use this on any emotional or physical problem by customizing it with an appropriate Setup Statement and Reminder Phrase. Be persistent until all parts of the problem have vanished. Try it on anything and everything! It either works or it does no harm.

Basic Technique

Make a note (mental or written) of what specific problem is bothering you at this time. Rate how much it is affecting you on a scale from 0 to 10, with zero being no effect and ten the greatest effect imaginable.

1. **The Setup:** Make the following statement or a similar statement while continuously tapping (or massaging) the collarbone area with two or three fingers (you can use one or two hands): "Even though I have this [state specific problem], I deeply and completely accept myself the way I am."

2. **The Sequence:** (Repeat 3 times) With two or three fingers or the whole hand, tap five times (or massage an equal amount of time) on each of the following energy points while repeating a one or two word Reminder Phrase to keep you focused on your specific problem. Under the eyes, collar bone, four inches under the arm pit on your left side, and then, with hands intertwined (like a teepee), rub the edge of your fingers and thumbs together. Repeat this three times and then recheck your 0 to 10 level. The ideal goal is to repeat until you are at zero. See Figure 1.

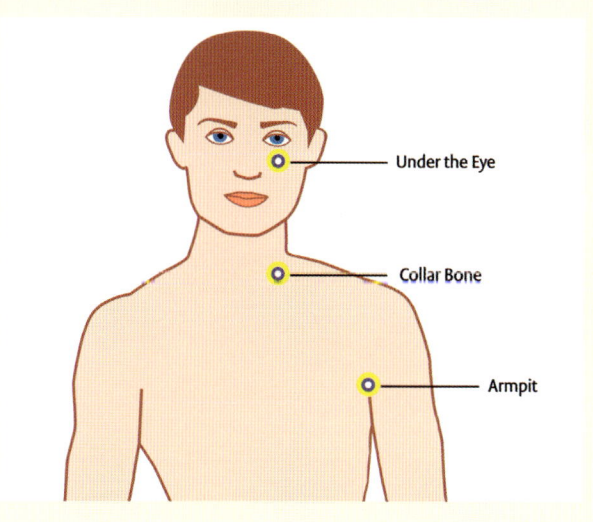

FIGURE 1

3. **The sequence is terminated.** Rate again how much the original problem is affecting you on the scale from 0 to 10. If there is still a problem, repeat Step 1 and 2 until you reach a zero.

Note: In subsequent rounds "The Setup Affirmation" is adjusted to reflect that you are addressing the remaining parts of the problem, i.e. *Even though I still [state the problem], I deeply and completely, etc.*

SOURCE: DR. C. E. "BUZZ" JOHNSON, BUZJOHNS@YAHOO.COM

Appendix E:
Suggested Reading List

Ask and It Is Given by Esther and Jerry Hicks

Freedom From Fear Forever by James Durlasher

Instant Emotional Healing by Peter Lambrou and George Pratt

Letter to Robin: A Mini Course in Pendulum Dowsing by Walt Woods

MAP: The Co-Creative White Brotherhood Medical Assistance Program by MacHaelle S. Wright

Path of Empowerment by Barbara Marciniak

The Pendulum Kit by Sig Lonegren

The Power of Intention by Wayne Dyer

Power vs. Force by David Hawkins

You Can Heal Your Life by Louise Hay

Appendix F:

The Grand Invocation

From the point of Light within the Mind of God,
Light now stream forth into the minds of humanity.
The Kingdom of Light has now emerged on earth.

From the Point of Love within the heart of God,
Love streams forth into the hearts of all.
The Light has returned to Earth.

From the center where the Will of God is known,
Divine purpose guides the Will of humanity,
The purpose which the Masters know and serve.

From the Center we call the Human Race,
The plan of Love and Light now governs.
Having forever sealed the door where darkness dwells.

Divine Light and Love has restored the plan on earth.

And so it is!

Appendix G: Disclaimer

The glyphs in this book represent the power of prayer. They should not be construed as orthodox or alternative medicine, diagnostic tools, or medical devices for the treatment of any type of disease or illness. The prayer energy from the glyphs helps enable the user to heal themselves, which is their right to do. These glyphs should not replace or interfere with any type of medical treatment. In the case of any serious illness, always consult a qualified medical practitioner.

Assistance Program for Children
Children are the Future

We are helping them get from here…

to here…

Happiness Orphanage - Kathmandu, Nepal

All over the world there are children sleeping in streets, doorways and under cardboard boxes, surviving by eating leftover food, doing heavy manual labor, selling trinkets, begging and stealing. Children are the future of their country, and of the world. One step at a time they can be helped to believe in their ability to create a better life for themselves and their community. It is not our goal to change their spiritual beliefs, only to help them realize how wonderful and powerful they are and that they can make a difference. A good example is an orphanage in Nepal that *Holy Ground Farm* is assisting.

100% of all donations are used to support programs for children.